MICROSOFT
EXCEL®
MADE EASY

2018-19 EDITION

ROB HAWKINS

FLAME TREE
PUBLISHING

CONTENTS

New to Excel? Need to brush up on your spreadsheet skills? This is the place to start. This chapter includes a comprehensive list of spreadsheet jargon, examples of how Excel can be used, and a history of how Excel and spreadsheets have developed. There is an illustrated guide to what's on the Excel screen and no-nonsense instructions on the best ways of getting started, including opening files, saving work, finding files, moving around a spreadsheet and moving between worksheets.

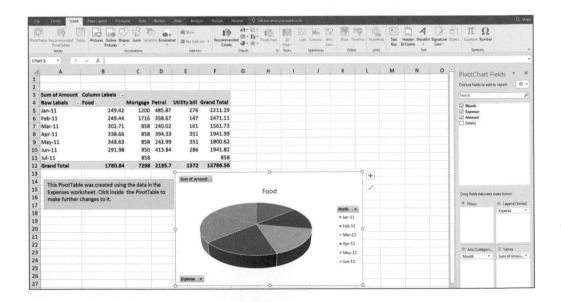

Excel has many data-entry features and all are explained in this chapter. Find out how to correctly enter and amend data, as well all the shortcuts available to help save time. This chapter outlines quick techniques for selecting and copying cells, pasting methods, and fast ways of editing data, including deleting, altering sizes and formatting. Learn how to change cell colours with Conditional Formatting and follow some comprehensive step-by-step guides to see how else this feature can be used.

Spreadsheets containing large amounts of data can often be difficult to understand, so this chapter explains some of the tools available in Excel that can help decipher thousands of rows of information. Excel can dissect calculations and explain how they have been constructed. Useful tools – including freezing panes, multiple views, Outline, Filter, Subtotal, Sort and PivotTables – are all explained in detail, and there are step-by-step guides to walk you through some of the main features.

Calculations are one of the main features of Excel and form the core purpose of the program. This chapter is part practical and part reference, with clear instructions on how to create calculations and the rules that accompany them, followed by information on using functions such as SUM, IF and Vlookup. Easy-to-follow guides show how particular features work, and at the end of the chapter is a list of quick-reference definitions.

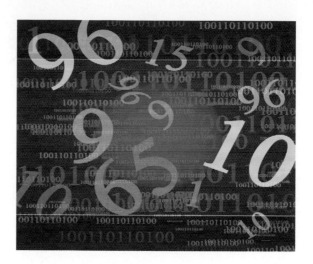

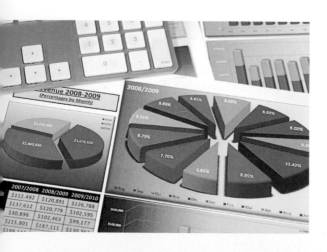

Excel data often needs to be presented in an efficient and accessible way. This chapter covers the tools in Excel that can be used to help forecast or summarize results, illustrate sales figures and format data for presentations. It will show you how to get to grips with forecasting, using a cash-flow forecast as an example. This section also explains how to consolidate large quantities of data, customize charts, and illustrate and print out your report or presentation.

MISTAKES AND ERRORS.......................208

This chapter will help you anticipate the problems sometimes experienced with Excel, and explains how to resolve them if they do occur. It offers straightforward instructions on how Excel can help to reduce errors and how to use the tools available to improve the accuracy of data, as well the facilities to check it. Data Validation, Conditional Formatting and Formula Auditing are all covered in depth, and the chapter concludes with a troubleshooting checklist and some 'afraid-to-ask' questions.

EXTRA PRACTICE 244

One of the best ways of becoming an expert in Excel is to create different spreadsheets and practise using different features. This chapter contains several step-by-step guides on using specific features in Excel. These exercises range from calculating a loan to downloading a bank statement. You can enter your own data, or you can download an Excel file that features sample data and examples.

INTRODUCTION

Since Microsoft Excel first appeared in 1985, this computerized spreadsheet has gradually become a market leader. Over the years it has evolved to incorporate an increasing number of features that can be confusing to beginners and more experienced users alike. So, whether you've never set eyes on a spreadsheet before or have used one regularly for many years, this book provides a practical education in the use of Excel, and resolves many of the frustrating points that often become assumed knowledge with an established computer program.

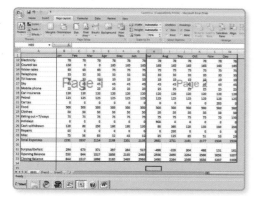

EXCEL HAS EVOLVED

Excel can be used for a wide range of purposes. Traditionally, its main function was for accounting and storing financial data. However, over the years the program has become more sophisticated, and many people have realized the benefit of using it for creating presentations and reports, with colourful charts and summarized totals for sales results. Data input can be made easy and error-free, saving hours of typing time and correcting mistakes. There are also plenty of uses for Excel at home, including downloading bank statements, listing valuables for a home insurance policy and completing a self-assessment tax return.

NEED TO KNOW

While the ideas for applying Excel keep on growing, understanding how to use it and ensuring the accuracy of the end result can be problematic. Consequently, it is often quicker to grab a calculator or use another computer program. This book provides practical advice so that you don't feel the need to go elsewhere. Excel is not one of those programs that can be opened for the first time and 10 minutes later you have a sales analysis report, complete with forecasted figures, charts and a summary table for the last 10 years. You need to know how to create this type of analysis – a subject covered in this book. To avoid moments of frustration and confusion, it

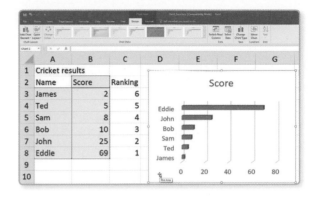

is also essential to understand the terminology used by Excel's creators, so to help you out we have defined most of the jargon you will come across when using Excel and spreadsheets in general.

VERSIONS COVERED

Since its launch in 1985, Excel has been updated more than a dozen times and in 2007, Microsoft made some extensive alterations to the look of the program. This book covers versions of Excel ranging from 4.0a (released in 1992) to Excel 2016, which has had security updates for 2017 and 2018. Whether you're attempting to transfer from Excel 2000 to 2010, or remaining faithful to the Excel 5.0 that you bought back in 1993, this book states which information applies to which version of Excel, but caters for every version released since 1992. Of course, Microsoft continues to release ongoing security updates and there is a 2019 update of Office – the software family that includes Excel – but this brings new features that focus mainly on connectivity to the Cloud and online functionality. This book will take you through all the core uses you need to know for all the versions.

SEVEN CHAPTERS

The contents of this book are split into seven chapters, beginning with some simple explanations about how Excel can be used and what all the jargon means. The second chapter covers quick techniques for inputting data, copying, formatting and deleting. Chapter 3 launches into large spreadsheets, explaining how to use Excel's features to analyse long lists of data. Chapter 4 covers one of Excel's traditional uses – calculations. Chapter 5 is task-specific for those wanting to use Excel to forecast sales figures or expenditure, produce reports or create presentations. Chapter 6 tackles problems users can face with Excel, outlining typical errors and explaining how to resolve them and reduce the risk of them occurring. The final chapter is task-specific, offering step-by-step guides to creating an expenses list, downloading a bank statement and calculating a loan.

SMALL CHUNKS

Each chapter is divided into manageable chunks of information about Excel and its features. You do not need to read these from start to finish. Rather, the sections are task-oriented so they can be read and put into practice on their own according to your needs. For example,if you are just trying to find the best way of documenting and managing your household expenses, you can go right to that section and follow the instructions there. Within each chapter, a range of Hot Tips also provide useful hints linked to the subjects under discussion.

STEP BY STEP

Throughout the book there are step-by-step guides covering everything from calculating a loan or investment to downloading a bank statement, creating a cash-flow forecast to listing household expenses. Specific Excel features such as PivotTables, Subtotals, Conditional Formatting, Vlookups, Charts, Data Validation and AutoFilter are all covered in the practical guides in the relevant chapters.

DOWNLOAD AND PRACTISE

If you want to practise with Excel using the same data shown in this book, go to the publisher's website at http://www.flametreepublishing.com/samples and download the file Excel_Exercises.xls. This file contains ten worksheets with fictitious data relating to the lsubjects covered in the book (references are made to these files where appropriate).

HELP!

If you're stuck on a particular topic, please email Flame Tree Publishing at support@ flametreepublishing.com. While we cannot operate a 24-hour helpline for all your Excel needs, we will answer your query via email.

UNDERSTAND MORE, ACHIEVE MORE

The contents of this book have been researched through 20 years of delivering Excel training courses, using versions as early as 5.0 and as up-to-date as 2016. The author, Rob Hawkins, has taught hundreds of people to use Excel at a variety of levels, ranging from absolute beginners to expert programmers, data analysts and engineers. He has also completed consultancy contracts where Excel has been used within the steel industry and retail market.

The use of Excel, and indeed many computer programs, is very different to what it was 20 years ago, when people were still familiarizing themselves with often quite simple functions. Despite today's more widespread proficiency with computers and higher skill levels in programs such as Excel, there will always be gaps in a user's knowledge. Many people still struggle with the rules of calculations, effectively copying data, understanding functions such as a Vlookup or IF and how a PivotTable can be used. All these issues – and more – are covered clearly and concisely in this book. The correct use of Excel can shave hours off a working week and improve the efficiency of your household administration. Using this book will show you how easy Excel really can be.

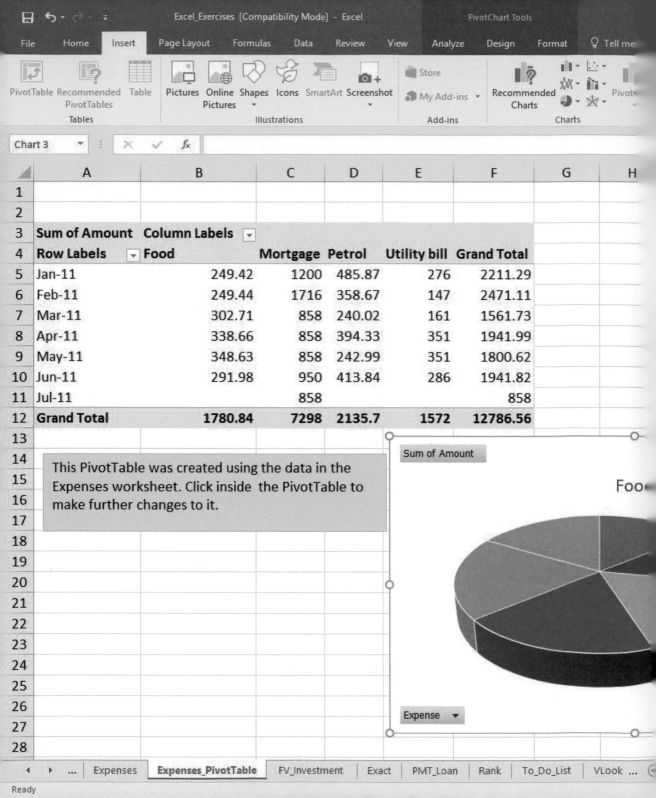

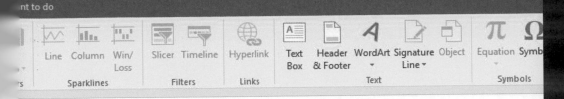

Sign in

Line	Column	Win/Loss		Slicer	Timeline	Hyperlink		Text Box	Header & Footer	WordArt	Signature Line	Object		Equation	Symb
	Sparklines				Filters		Links			Text				Symbols	

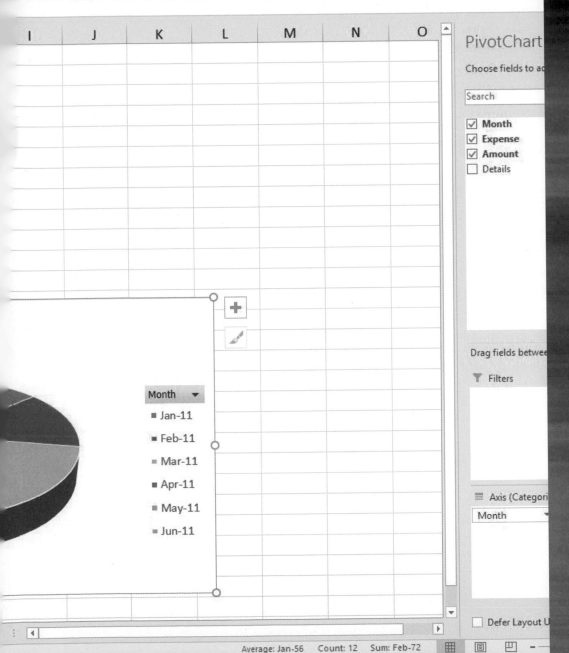

PivotChart

Choose fields to a

Search

☑ **Month**
☑ **Expense**
☑ **Amount**
☐ Details

Drag fields betwee

▼ Filters

▤ Axis (Categori

Month ▼

Month ▼
■ Jan-11
■ Feb-11
■ Mar-11
■ Apr-11
■ May-11
■ Jun-11

☐ Defer Layout U

Average: Jan-56   Count: 12   Sum: Feb-72

WHAT IS EXCEL?

EXCEL JARGON

Excel can seem more confusing than it really is if you don't know the meaning of some of the technical terms used within the program, so this section provides a quick reference guide to Excel's jargon.

SPREADSHEET

A spreadsheet is quite literally a method of spreading information across a sheet. Consequently, a computer spreadsheet resembles a piece of paper with a grid format printed on it. The grid format makes it easy to enter information in a logical manner – down or across the spreadsheet – and provides a simple way of locating that information.

Spreadies

Programs such as Excel are referred to as spreadsheet programs, and the files they use are known as spreadsheets. Many people also call a single page or sheet in a file a spreadsheet, although these are properly known as worksheets. Those who use spreadsheets a lot sometimes refer to them as 'spreadies'.

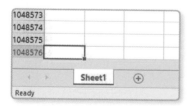

Above: Excel 2007 and later versions have over one million rows in each worksheet.

ROWS

The lines or cells across a spreadsheet are known as rows. Each row is identified by a row number, which is displayed down the left side of the screen. The number of rows in each worksheet varies according to the version of Excel you are using, but they are all based on a mathematical formula that starts at 1 and doubles the value each time. This is characteristic of many computer values, including memory and hard-disk space. If you start at 1 and keep doubling the figures, you will arrive at familiar values such as 256, 512, 1,024 and 2,048.

Ever-Increasing Numbers

Excel's rows extended to 8,192 and 16,384 in the early 1990s, then hit 65,536 with Excel 97. Excel 2007 and later versions have broken into the millions with a staggering 1,048,576 rows! This might appear excessive, but in fact this number of rows can easily be filled by importing a list of sales results, for example, or names and addresses for a city or region.

Hot Tip

For sample worksheets, visit www.flametreepublishing.com/samples and download the Excel_Exercises.xls workbook file.

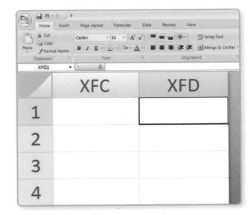

Above: There are 16,384 columns in a worksheet for Excel 2007–2016.

COLUMNS

The cells down a spreadsheet are called columns and are identified by a series of alphabetically ordered letters across the top of the worksheet. They run from A to Z, then move on to AA, AB, AC to AZ, followed by BA, BB, BC, and so on. Prior to the release of Excel 2007, the majority of versions of Excel had 256 columns, which finished at IV. Excel 2007 and later versions have 16,384 columns, finishing at XFD.

CELLS

A particular point in the grid of a spreadsheet is referred to as a cell. The location is identified by a cell reference, such as B20 or A10. For example, A10 refers to column A and row number 10. Excel has adopted this style of cell referencing as a default setting (a standard setting), although other methods have been used and are still available, such as column and row numbers (e.g. R5C6 locates the cell in the fifth row and sixth column).

WORKBOOK

A workbook is simply the name for an Excel file that contains one or more spreadsheet pages (or worksheets). The terms 'file' and 'workbook' are interchangeable in Excel.

Hot Tip

Providing your computer doesn't run out of memory, there's no limit to the number of sheets you can have in a workbook in Excel 2010 and later versions.

WORKSHEET

A single page of an Excel spreadsheet is known as a worksheet. Each worksheet is displayed as a series of tabs near the bottom left of the active page. They are like the pages of a book.

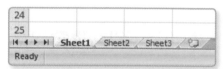

Above: Worksheets are the pages of an Excel workbook and are displayed near the bottom left corner of the screen.

RIBBON

Excel 2007 and later versions use toolbar ribbons instead of the traditional drop-down menus and toolbar buttons. There is still a menu bar, with familiar tabs such as Insert and View, but when you click on one of these tabs, a row of toolbar buttons appears below in a feature known as a ribbon.

Hot Tip

Excel 2007–2016's ribbon can be minimized and maximized by holding down the Ctrl key on the keyboard and pressing F1.

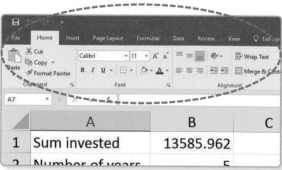

Above: Excel 2007 and later versions use a ribbon to display toolbar buttons and menu options; a series of ribbon tabs can be seen across the top of the screen.

USES FOR EXCEL

Excel has evolved from being a calculations-based program used mainly by accountants and statisticians, to offering a wide variety of functions that almost everyone will find useful. These include downloading and storing bank statements, listing household valuables and creating claims forms. Below are some examples of how Excel can be used.

BANK AND CREDIT CARD STATEMENTS

Most of the major banks, building societies and financial institutions provide online banking with the facility to download bank statements. These statements are often saved in a

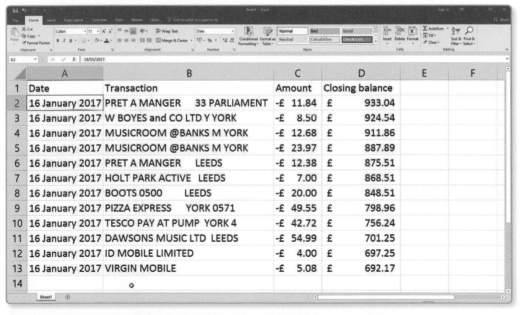

Above: Excel can be used to store downloaded bank statements and help keep track of payments in and out.

file format that can be opened in Excel (comma separated values or CSV, text or TXT, or an Excel file). Once opened, the bank statement is usually presented as a four- or five-column list, with headings for the date of each transaction, details or a description of the transaction, its value (sometimes payments out are displayed as negative values) and the closing balance.

Hot Tip

More information on downloading bank statements is covered on pages 105 and 248.

Create Your Own

If you find that your online bank statement is not available in any of these formats, it may still be possible to copy and paste it into an Excel document from the version viewed on screen. Excel can sort and filter the data, and the information can also be added to older statements to provide one continuous document for a particular account.

MILEAGE CLAIM FORMS

Excel is very useful for time-saving calculations, which makes filling in forms such as expenses or mileage claims a lot faster and error-free. The vast assortment of formatting tools (including colours, borders, shading) means you can also make a claim form look professional and use it as an official document at work, avoiding the need to buy or custom print expensive stationery.

SELF-ASSESSMENT

If you're one of the many millions of people who have to complete a tax return every year, then Excel can save on time and also help with planning. Most tax returns can be completed online, but it is important to make sure that the figures are entered correctly and that the final calculation is correct. Inputting your figures in Excel before including them in your tax return will make sure you've got it right – and that you don't end up paying too much tax!

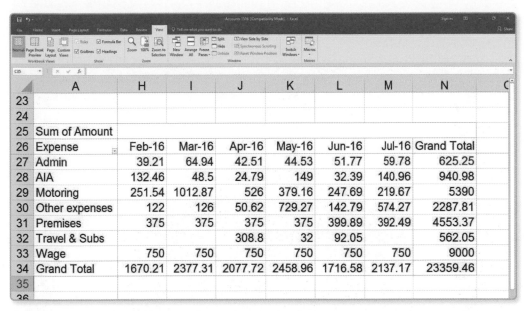

	A	H	I	J	K	L	M	N	C
23									
24									
25	Sum of Amount								
26	Expense	Feb-16	Mar-16	Apr-16	May-16	Jun-16	Jul-16	Grand Total	
27	Admin	39.21	64.94	42.51	44.53	51.77	59.78	625.25	
28	AIA	132.46	48.5	24.79	149	32.39	140.96	940.98	
29	Motoring	251.54	1012.87	526	379.16	247.69	219.67	5390	
30	Other expenses	122	126	50.62	729.27	142.79	574.27	2287.81	
31	Premises	375	375	375	375	399.89	392.49	4553.37	
32	Travel & Subs			308.8	32	92.05		562.05	
33	Wage	750	750	750	750	750	750	9000	
34	Grand Total	1670.21	2377.31	2077.72	2458.96	1716.58	2137.17	23359.46	
35									
36									

Above: If you're self-employed, Excel can be very useful for keeping track of your accounts and helping you complete your self-assessment tax return.

KNOW YOUR VALUABLES

Most household, business and personal insurance policies require an estimated value for belongings and valuables. Many people find that when they add all this up, it is far more than they had thought it would be. Excel can not only help you add up the cost of your possessions, it can also help you keep track of their value and display a running total as more items are added to the list. This is covered in greater depth in Chapter 3.

TRACK YOUR WARRANTIES

How many of us know when the manufacturer's guarantee on our oven runs out, or can remember whether or not we bought the extended warranty on our television? If a device stops working when it is still under warranty, where are the details of where you bought it

and who to call? List all this information in Excel and not only will it be instantly accessible when you need it, but you can also decide whether or not to renew a warranty when the time comes.

Hot Tip

Including details on when items were purchased will also help you compare new-for-old insurance policies and those that pay the second-hand value.

PRICE COMPARISONS

Whether you are planning a holiday or shopping around for an insurance policy, Excel can come in useful for comparing quotes and figuring out what you get for your money. Quotes for car insurance, for example, can be listed in Excel and compared at a glance to see which ones include a courtesy car, no-claims bonus protection and how much the voluntary excess costs. Excel lets you decide what headings you want for the list and offers plenty of space to spread the list across a worksheet.

THINGS TO DO

Excel isn't just for storing financial information. It can be used for something as simple as a list of jobs to do at home (fix the dripping tap, paint the spare room, take the car for an MOT test etc.). There are some useful features in Excel to help you colour-code jobs according to their level of urgency and then sort them in order of their colours. Chapter 3 goes into more detail on this subject, and includes a step-by-step guide to creating your own to-do list in Excel.

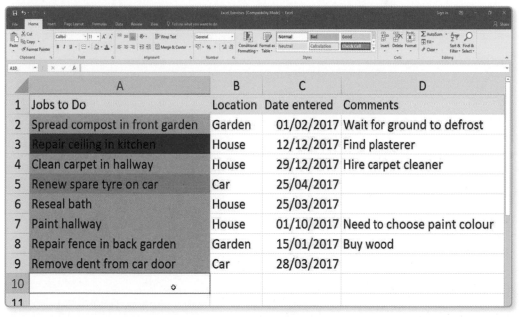

Above: Excel is useful for making a to-do list of jobs and colour-coding them according to their level of urgency.

A HISTORY OF EXCEL AND SPREADSHEETS

Although Excel first appeared in the 1980s, spreadsheets themselves have been in use since the 1960s. This section provides a brief history of spreadsheets and how they have evolved since their early days. It also gives a checklist of the different versions of Excel.

EARLY SPREADSHEETS

The first computer-based spreadsheets were not created for personal computing, but to run on large corporate mainframe computers for accounting purposes. Professor Richard Mattessich was the man behind the development of a mainframe-based spreadsheet, which first emerged in 1961, and this was eventually used by the likes of Bell Canada, AT&T and General Motors. During the late 1970s, a spreadsheet program called VisiCalc (visible calculator) was developed. This gained popularity in the 1980s, until Lotus 123 emerged and became a leading brand, with many features that are still available today. The spreadsheet program Quattro Pro also appeared in the 1980s.

The Rise of Excel

In the early 1990s, Lotus 123 was – in many people's opinion – the best spreadsheet program available and was the market leader. However, in the mid-1980s, Microsoft had launched a rival spreadsheet called Excel for the Apple Macintosh computer; it became available for the PC and Windows in 1987 (Excel version 2.0). Despite Lotus 123 owning VisiCalc and having the necessary supporting software (for example, Lotus Notes was an all-in-one package like Microsoft Office), Excel was the only spreadsheet that could be run through Microsoft Windows until 1992. Lotus 123 remained popular throughout the 1990s, but today it has been overtaken in the market by Excel.

VERSIONS OF EXCEL

The table below and overleaf outlines the development of Excel.

Year	Excel version	Comments
1985	1.0	Available only for Apple Mac.
1987	2.0	Available for PC with MS-DOS operating system.
1987	3.0	Available for PC with Windows operating system.
1989	2.2	Available only for Apple Mac.
1990	3.0	Available only for Apple Mac.
1992	4.0 and 4.0a	Launched in January 1992 and available for PC, with Windows 3.11. 4.0a available in November 1992.
1993	5.0	Available for PC with Windows 3.11 featuring several improvements over version 4.0a.
1995	7.0/95	Available for PC with Windows 95 or NT; new features included better integration with other Microsoft programs.

Year	Excel version	Comments
1997	8.0/97	Available for PC with Windows 95 and packaged under Office '97. New features included an Office Assistant help feature.
2000	2000	Packaged under Office 2000.
2002	2002	Available as part of Office 2002. New features included a Task Pane and better analysis tools.
2003	2003	Available as part of Office 2003.
2007	2007	A completely revised version of Excel with a new look and lots of new features. An end to menu bars and toolbars.
2010	2010	Similar to Excel 2007, but with some new features and improvements.
2013	2013	Similar to Excel 2010, but with additional features and more functions.
2016	2016	Similar layout to 2010/2013, but with new features including forecasting functions and more chart types.

Above: To find which version of Excel you have, click on the Help menu if this is displayed and choose About Microsoft Excel, or click on the File menu, choose Account and select About Excel.

Which Version Do I Have?

Not sure which version of Excel you have? If you can see a Help menu near the top middle of the screen, then click on it and choose About Microsoft Excel. A box will appear displaying the version of Excel at the top. If you cannot see a Help menu, you have Excel 2007 or or a later version, so click on the question mark at the top right corner of the screen to activate Help. A separate box will appear, displaying the version of Excel you are using.

Hot Tip

In 1982, Microsoft launched a spreadsheet called Multiplan, aimed at competing with VisiCalc.

EXCEL ON THE MACINTOSH

Although the Apple Macintosh computer has its own operating system, Microsoft has developed Excel to work in much the same way as it does on a Windows platform. Excel for Windows and Excel for the Mac share a common interface and functionality, making it easier for companies to support both platforms, and file compatibility between the two operating systems is very high, enabling users to share files between PCs and Macs. This book has been written for all versions of Excel for the PC, but most of the information can be applied to the Apple Mac. See also pages 33–34 for more on the differences between PCs and Macs.

ON THE SCREEN

The main screen in Excel can seem bewildering if you don't know what you're looking for and don't recognize any of the symbols on it. The following pages provide detailed explanations of the various aspects of the Excel screen, ranging from the older editions to the latest 2007–2016 versions.

EXCEL PRE-2007 ON THE PC

1   **Title bar:** The title bar appears at the top of all Microsoft applications. It displays the name of the application and the current workbook on the left-hand side, and contains control buttons to make changes to the window on the right-hand side.

2   **Minimize button:** The minimize button on the title bar will reduce the Excel window and display it as a button on the Windows taskbar. The minimize button on the menu bar will minimize the current workbook.

3   **Maximize/Restore button:** The maximize button (which looks like a single box) on the title bar will enlarge the Excel window to the full size of the screen. The maximize button on the menu bar will maximize the workbook window inside Excel. If this button looks like two boxes (restore) then clicking on it will reduce the size of Excel.

4   **Close button:** The close button on the title bar will close Excel. The close button on the menu bar will close the current workbook.

5   **Menu bar:** The menu bar provides a range of options for creating and maintaining your workbook. By clicking on a menu name (File, Edit, etc.), a drop-down menu will appear.

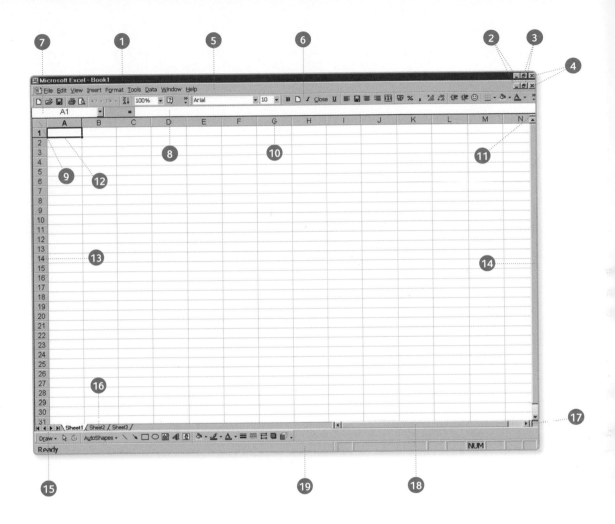

6 **Excel toolbar**: This provides a full range of separate toolbars, each containing a number of buttons. These buttons offer shortcuts to commonly used features.

7 **Name box**: The name box displays the cell address or name of the currently selected cell. The drop-down box provides a list of all the named cells within the worksheet.

8   **Formula bar**: The formula bar shows the contents of the selected cell. If it cannot be seen, click on the View menu and make sure there's a tick mark against Formula bar.

9   **Select-all button**: When you click on the select-all button, all the cells in the worksheet are selected.

10   **Column headings**: There are 256 columns in a worksheet, labelled A through to IV. The column heading displays the labels from A to Z, then AA to AZ, BA to BZ, and so on through to IV. Clicking on a column heading selects the whole of that column.

11   **Horizontal split box**: This split box can be used to divide the window horizontally so that you can view two areas of the worksheet at the same time. Drag the split box along the scroll bar to where you want the window split.

12   **Active cell indicator**: You can see which cell is active because it has a dark border around it. This is known as the active cell indicator, and it has a small black square in the bottom right-hand corner.

13   **Row headings**: There are 65,536 rows within each worksheet. The row headings are displayed down the left side of the screen.

14   **Vertical scroll bar**: The vertical scroll bar allows you to scroll up and down through the rows of the worksheet.

15   **Tab scroll buttons**: The tab scroll buttons are used to scroll the sheet tabs when some of them cannot be seen. Right-click on any of these buttons to see a full list of them.

16   **Sheet tabs**: The sheet tabs display the names of the worksheets that make up the current workbook. To make a sheet active, click on the sheet tab.

17 **Vertical split box**: This split box can be used to divide the window vertically so that you can view two areas of the worksheet at the same time. Drag the split box down the scroll bar to where you want the window split.

18 **Horizontal scroll bar**: The horizontal scroll bar allows you to scroll left and right through the columns of the worksheet.

19 **Status bar**: The left side of the status bar displays the current command or operation and the right side displays the status of the Num Lock, Caps Lock and Scroll Lock keys. If you do not want the status bar displayed, click on the View menu and uncheck the Status Bar option.

EXCEL 2007-2016 ON THE PC

The screen for Excel 2007–2016 looks very different to that of earlier versions. However, there are several similarities including scroll bars, minimize and maximize buttons, the formula bar and status bar. New features include the replacement of the menu bar and toolbar buttons with a selection of ribbons.

1 **Title bar**: The title bar appears at the top of all Microsoft applications. It displays the name of the application and the current workbook.

2 **Quick access toolbar**: This toolbar is usually displayed at the top left corner of the screen, but it can be moved further down below the ribbon. The quick access toolbar displays some of the commonly used buttons, such as Open, Save, Undo and Print. Buttons can be added and removed by clicking on its drop-down arrow.

3 **Minimize button**: The minimize button on the title bar will reduce the Excel window and display it as a button on the Windows taskbar. In Excel 2007–2010, the minimize button on the menu bar will minimize the current workbook.

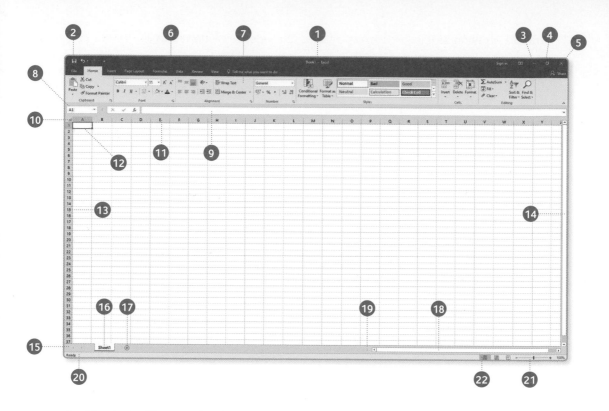

4   Maximize/Restore button: If this button looks like a single box, then clicking on it will enlarge the Excel page to the full size of the screen (maximize). If there are two boxes (restore), then clicking on it will reduce the Excel window so other programs and the desktop can be seen.

5   Close button: The close button on the title bar will close Excel. In Excel 2007–2010, the close button below it will close the current workbook.

6   Ribbon tabs: The tabs near the top of the screen labelled File, Home, Insert, Page Layout, Formulas, Data, Review and View are used to open different ribbons below. These ribbons contain toolbar buttons associated with each ribbon tab.

7   **Ribbon:** A ribbon contains a series of buttons, just like a traditional toolbar. Each set of ribbon buttons is associated with its ribbon tab. The ribbon can be minimized and maximized by right-clicking on it and selecting Minimize Ribbon or Collapse Ribbon (if there is a tick mark against this option it will maximize).

8   **Name box:** The name box displays the cell address – the name of the currently selected cell. The drop-down box provides a list of all the named cells within the worksheet.

9   **Formula bar:** The formula bar displays the contents of the selected cell.

10 **Select-all button:** When you click on the select-all button, the entire worksheet is selected.

11 **Column headings:** The column headings display the column labels from A to Z, then AA to AZ, BA to BZ, and so on. Excel 2007–2016 have 16,384 columns, which end at XFD.

12 **Active cell indicator:** A dark border identifies the selected cell. This is known as the active cell indicator, and it can be moved to select other cells by using the mouse or arrow keys on the keyboard.

13 **Row headings:** The row headings display the row numbers in a spreadsheet and are listed down the left side of the screen. Excel 2007–2016 have 1,048,576 rows.

14 **Vertical scroll bar:** The vertical scroll bar allows you to scroll up and down through the rows of the worksheet.

15 **Tab scroll buttons:** The tab scroll buttons are used to scroll the sheet tabs if some of them are not visible. Right click on any of these buttons for a list of worksheets.

16 **Sheet tabs:** The sheet tabs display the names of the worksheets that make up the open workbook. By default, each new workbook contains one or three sheets, depending on the version of Excel. A workbook can contain an unlimited number of sheets, however.

17 Insert worksheet: Click on this button to the right of the sheet tabs to add a new worksheet to the Excel workbook instantly.

18 Horizontal scroll bar: The horizontal scroll bar allows you to scroll left and right through the columns of the worksheet.

19 Resize the horizontal scroll bar: The small up-turned rectangle or three vertical dots to the left of the horizontal scroll bar allows this scroll bar to be resized. Position the mouse pointer over it and when it changes to a cross with two arrows, drag the mouse left or right to resize the scroll bar. (Not available on Excel 15.0 for Mac.)

20 Status bar: The left side of the status bar displays the current command or operation, as well as advice on how to use a selected feature in Excel.

21 Zoom control: Drag the slider to zoom in and out of the spreadsheet. Click on the percentage value to open a Zoom dialogue box and change the settings.

22 Layouts: Click on the small buttons to change between views – Normal, Page Layout and Page Break Preview. These views are especially useful when printing spreadsheets.

Vertical and horizontal split boxes: This feature is only available in Excel 2010 and earlier versions (and Excel 15.0 for Mac). These little narrow boxes containing a line, one located at the top of the vertical scroll bar and the other at the righthand side of the horizontal scroll bar, can be used to divide the window horizontally or vertically so two areas of the worksheet can be viewed at the same time. Drag the split box along the scroll bar to where you want to split the window. To split the screen without using these boxes or in later versions of Excel, see pages 52–53.

Hot Tip

When using the zoom control, you can click on the plus (+) and minus (–) symbols as well as dragging the slider to zoom in and out.

EXCEL ON THE SCREEN – ON MACS

As we have said, most of the information in this book can easily be applied to Apple Macintosh computers too. As you can see from the following two screen shots, they are very similar – the numbered descriptions on pages 26–29 and 29–32 respectively correspond to the annotation here just as well, with only a few minor differences – for example, you'll notice the name of the application ('Excel') is on the 'menu bar', not the 'title bar'.

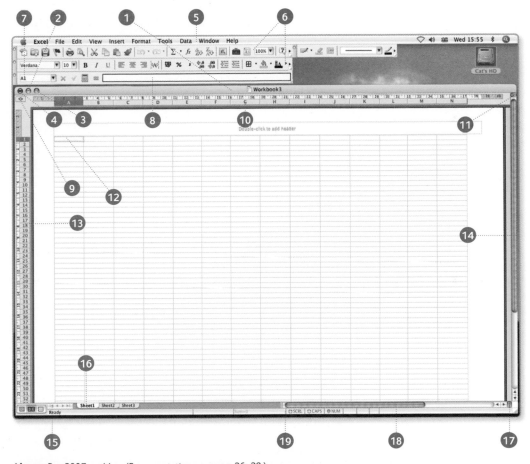

Above: Pre-2007 on Mac. (See annotation on pages 26–29.)

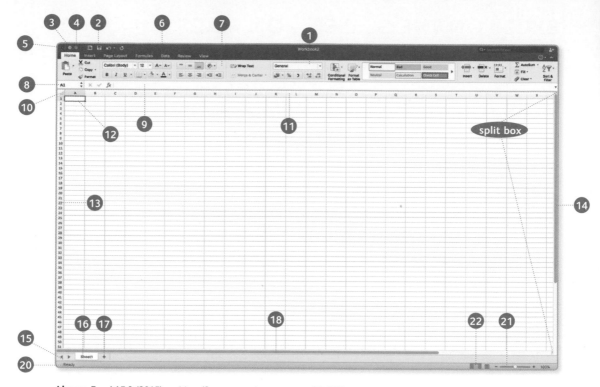

Above: Excel 15.0 (2015) on Mac. (See annotation on pages 29–32.)

A NOTE ON KEYBOARD DIFFERENCES

Any keyboard-related instructions in this book are based on using a keyboard connected to a PC, but depending on the type of keyboard you are using, you may find some differences. Similarly, if you are using an Apple Mac, there are a few different keys. For example, most importantly, the Ctrl key on the PC is the Command (Apple) key on the Apple Mac (not the one labelled 'Ctrl' confusingly!). The Page Up/Down keys on the PC are usually labelled by an up/down arrow with two short horizontal lines on the Apple Mac. Right clicking is also different on an Apple Mac to the PC – hold down the Ctrl key and click instead. Some of the function (F) keys may also not work as described – especially in Mac OS X version 10.3 and later where there can be a conflict with the default key assignments for the Exposé feature.

GETTING STARTED IN EXCEL

Now that you are familiar with what you can see on screen when you open Excel, it's time to get to grips with some basic functions. There are many shortcuts and quick techniques for opening, closing and saving Excel files, and for making sure files are not lost.

OPENING AND CLOSING EXCEL

There are several ways of opening Excel and there are no right or wrong methods. However, it's worth trying them all to see which one is the fastest and easiest for you.

Opening Excel

→ **Start menu or Windows button:** Click on the Start menu or Windows button at the bottom left corner of the screen and you may find Excel listed in the menu that pops up. If not, scroll down or select Programs or All Programs and look for it on the sub-menu that appears. If it's not there, select Microsoft Office and click on Excel in the next sub-menu.

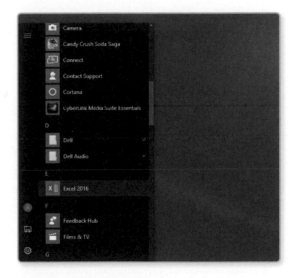

→ **Taskbar:** If Excel is displayed as a small green icon (symbol) near the bottom left of the screen, then click on it once with the mouse to open the program.

Above: Excel can be opened via the Start menu or the Windows button at the bottom left. You may have to scroll down the list of programs or open a sub-menu to find it.

Above: Some keyboards have an Excel symbol displayed on one of the function keys – a quick way of opening the program.

➔ **Open an Excel file**: Instead of opening Excel, you can open an Excel file to automatically open the program. Excel files are usually found via My Computer or My Documents.

➔ **Keyboard shortcut**: Some keyboards have an Excel symbol on one of the Function keys (e.g. F3, above), which opens Excel. You may have to hold down another key to activate these keyboard features.

> ## Hot Tip
> If you are about to close down your computer and have several programs open, then as long as you've saved any open files, just click on the Start or Windows button and choose Turn Off Computer or Shutdown.

Closing Excel

➔ **File menu**: Click on the File menu or ribbon tab in Excel and select Exit or Close (near the bottom of the menu that appears). If any Excel files have not been saved, you will be prompted to save them before the program closes.

File menu using the keyboard: Hold down the Alt key on the keyboard (near the bottom left), then press F. The File menu or ribbon menu will appear. Release all the keys on the keyboard, then press X for eXit or C for Close. Excel will close, but may prompt you to save changes to any unsaved files.

Close button: At the far top right corner of the screen there is an x-shaped button. Click on this to close Excel. Once again, you will be prompted to save any unsaved changes before the program closes. The x-shaped button below the one in the far top right corner will close an Excel file rather than the program (applies to Excel 2010 and earlier versions).

Keyboard shortcut: Hold down the Alt key on the keyboard (near the bottom left corner) and press the F4 key (above the numbers 4 and 5) once. Excel will close, but will ask you to save the changes for any files that have not been saved.

Right-click on the taskbar: When Excel is open, it appears on the taskbar along the bottom of the screen. It can be closed from here by right-clicking on this and choosing Close from the menu that appears. If any Excel files have not been saved, you will be asked whether you want to save them.

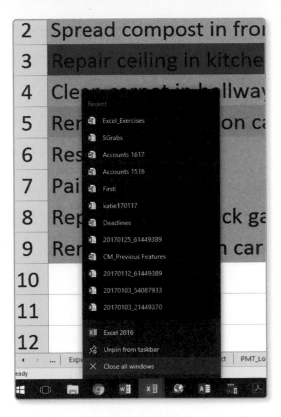

Above: Right click on the green Excel icon on the taskbar and choose Close all windows to close down Excel.

Hot Tip

Not sure if Excel is open or not? Look along the taskbar at the bottom of the screen to see if it's displayed. If so, click on it to display the program on screen.

OPENING NEW AND OLD FILES

Excel workbooks or files can be opened and created in a variety of ways using the keyboard, menus or toolbar buttons – or even a different program.

Creating a New Excel File

➔ **Keyboard**: Hold down the Ctrl key (near the bottom left corner of the keyboard), then press the letter N and release all the keyboard keys. A new Excel workbook (file) will appear on the screen.

➔ **Toolbar button (pre-2007)**: In Excel 2003 and earlier versions, search on the Standard toolbar in the top left of the screen for a toolbar button that looks like a white piece of paper. Click on this once to open a new Excel workbook.

➔ **Office button (2007)**: Click on the multicoloured Office button in the top left corner of the screen and choose New from the menu that appears. A New Workbook dialogue box will appear. Select Blank Workbook and click on the Create button.

Above: In Excel 2007–2016, there are a number of options on the File ribbon tab for creating a new Excel workbook.

Above: In Excel 2000 or earlier versions, click on the File menu and choose New; the dialogue box shown here will appear.

➔ **File ribbon (2010–2016):** Click on the File ribbon tab near the top left of the screen and choose New from the drop-down menu on the left side of the screen. A variety of options will appear. Look for Blank Workbook near the top left and select it to open a new workbook.

➔ **File menu (pre-2002):** Click on the File menu and choose New. A dialogue box will appear with a variety of options for opening a new workbook or an assortment of templates. Select Workbook and click on OK to open a new file in Excel.

➔ **File menu (2002 and 2003):** Click on the File menu and choose New. On the right-hand side of the screen is a bar called the task pane, including options for opening a new workbook. Select Blank Workbook to open an empty file in Excel.

Opening a Recently Used File

➔ **File menu (pre-2007):** Click on the File menu and look at the lower half of the menu. The last few Excel files that were opened will be listed. If the file you want is on the list, click on it to open.

Above: Click on the File menu in Excel 2003 and earlier versions for a list of previously opened Excel files.

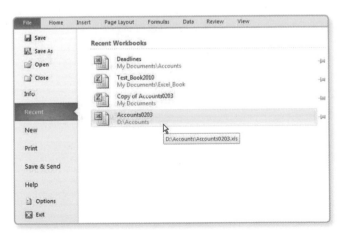

Above: Click on the Office button in Excel 2007 or the File ribbon tab in Excel 2010 and later versions. Select Open or Recent for a list of Excel files that have been opened.

Office button (2007): Click on the multicoloured Office button in the top left corner of the screen and a list of recently opened Excel files will be displayed, along with a number of menu options.

File ribbon (2010–2016): Click on the File ribbon tab near the top left corner of the screen. Select Recent or Open from the drop-down menu. The files that were last used in Excel will be displayed in the main part of the screen.

Hot Tip

Recently used files can be found in Windows Vista, XP and earlier versions by clicking on the Start menu at the bottom left corner of the screen and then selecting Documents.

Right click (2007 and and later versions): With Excel open, right-click on its icon in the taskbar along the bottom of the screen. A menu will appear with a section called Recent, showing the recently used Excel files.

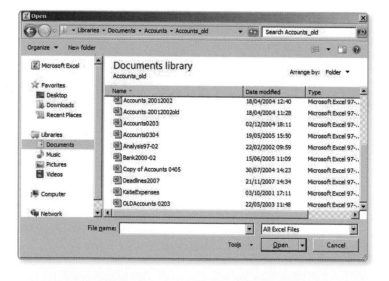

Opening an Old Excel File

You can use the Open dialogue box to locate an Excel file and open it. The appearance of this box varies depending on the version of Excel you are using, but the methods of opening folders and selecting an Excel file are the same.

Left: The Open dialogue box differs between the various versions of Excel, but is similar in how it can be used to search for and open files.

➔ **Keyboard shortcut**: Hold down the Ctrl key and press the letter O on the keyboard (not the zero), then release all the keys.

➔ **File menu (pre-2007)**: Click on the File menu and choose Open. The dialogue box will appear on the screen, allowing you to search for an Excel file and open it.

Above: In pre-2007 versions of Excel, click on the toolbar button that looks like a yellow folded piece of card to open an old file.

➔ **Office button (2007)**: Click on the multicoloured Office button in the top left corner of the screen and choose Open to activate the dialogue box.

➔ **File ribbon (2010–2016)**: Click on the File ribbon tab in the top left of the screen and choose Open or Browse. The dialogue box will appear.

➔ **Toolbar button (pre-2007)**: Find the yellow icon shaped like a folder being opened on the Standard toolbar in the top left of the screen. Hover the mouse over the icon and the word Open should appear. Click on the button and the dialogue box will appear, enabling you to locate an Excel file and open it.

➔ **Quick Access toolbar (2007–2016)**:
If a folder-shaped toolbar button is displayed near the top right corner of the screen, click on it to open the dialogue box. If there is no toolbar button, click on the drop-down triangle to the right of these buttons on the Quick Access toolbar and choose Open from the menu that appears.

Above: If the Open toolbar button isn't displayed on the quick access toolbar in Excel 2007–2016, it can be added via the drop-down menu.

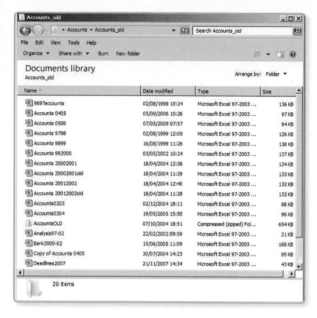

Above: Excel files can be opened using file viewers such as My Documents and Documents Library.

My Documents and Documents Library

If you are familiar with file viewers such as Windows Explorer, My Computer, My Documents and Documents Library, then you can open any Excel file from there without having to open the program itself. Opening an Excel file automatically opens the program.

What Did I Call It?

Forgotten what you called a file? All is not lost. The Open dialogue box also offers a number of search methods for both finding text in an Excel file and identifying its author. In pre-2007 versions, the search options are displayed near the bottom right corner of the Open dialogue box. There is also an Advanced button, which opens another dialogue box and allows you to search for specific words and values within your Excel files.

Finding Files in Excel 2007-2016

Excel 2007–2016 have a simpler but equally effective method of finding information within a file, using the search panel in the top right corner of the Open dialogue box. Just type in a keyword and Excel will search for it within the file names and contents of your documents.

Hot Tip

There is a search facility in Windows to help find lost Excel files. Click on the Start menu and select Search (for Windows 7, type in the search box on the Start menu).

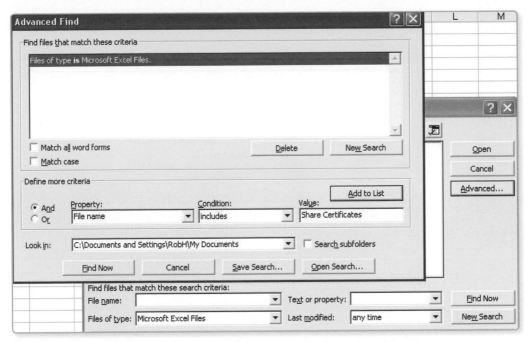

Above: Lost Excel files can be found using the Open dialogue box and its advanced search facilities.

SAVING FILES

Saving and resaving Excel files is quick and easy with keyboard shortcuts and toolbar buttons. It is good practice to save your Excel files regularly, but if a computer problem occurs, Excel has some recovery methods to ensure all is not lost.

First Save in Excel

If you are working in a new Excel file that hasn't been previously saved, then you will need to name and save it. The quickest way to do this is to hold down the Ctrl key on the keyboard and press the letter S. A Save As dialogue box will appear, allowing you to enter a name for your Excel file and choose a location in which to store it. In Excel 2013–2016, click on Browse or one of the locations displayed to open the Save As dialogue box.

Above: When a new Excel file is saved for the first time, the Save As dialogue box appears, allowing you to name the file and choose a location to store it in.

Resaving Excel Files

When working on a file and changing its contents, it is worthwhile resaving it every few minutes to avoid losing data should a computer problem occur. There are two quick ways to resave an Excel file:

→ **Keyboard shortcut**: Hold down the Ctrl key on the keyboard and press the letter S. You won't see much happening (in pre-2013 versions of Excel, a brown floppy disk symbol may briefly appear near the bottom of the screen), but the file will have been saved.

→ **Toolbar button**: Click on the Save toolbar button near the top left of the screen. This is the icon that looks like a floppy disk. The word Save will appear if you hover over it.

Changing File Names

You may want to change the name of an Excel file, or save a copy of it with a different name. Here's how to do this without overwriting the old file:

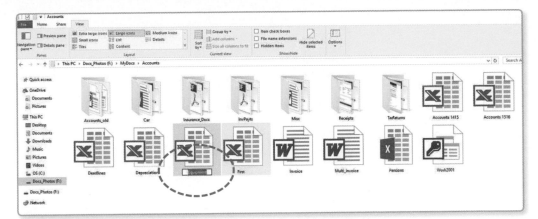

Above: Excel files can be quickly renamed in File viewers such as My Documents by using the F2 key on the keyboard.

- ➔ **Open the file you want to rename**
- ➔ **Press F12 on the keyboard**
- ➔ **Enter a new file name in the Save As dialogue box**
- ➔ **Choose a different storage location if required**
- ➔ **Click Save**

Saving Down

If you want to transfer an Excel file to another computer on which an earlier version of the program is installed, you'll need to save the file down to make sure it can be opened in the new location. To do this:

Right: Excel can save files for use with earlier versions of the program.

Hot Tip

File names can be quickly changed in My Documents, Windows Explorer and Documents Library. Just select a file, press F2 on the keyboard and type in a new name.

- Click on the File menu or File ribbon tab
- Choose Save As (or press F12 on the keyboard)
- Click on the drop-down triangle to the right of the Save As Type or File Type box
- From the file types listed, choose the version you need
- Rename the file if required
- Click Save

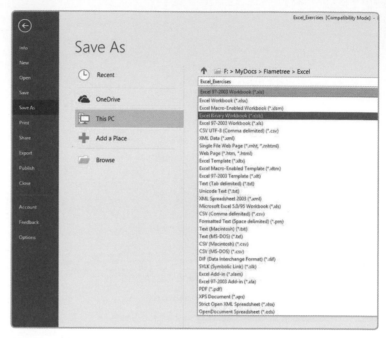

Above: Excel can save files for use with earlier versions of the program.

FILE EXTENSIONS

All file names have an extension to help identify the program in which it was created. This usually consists of three or four letters at the end of the file name and is separated from the file name with a full stop (e.g. Bank.xls). Pre-2007 versions of Excel have a .xls extension at the end of the file name, whereas files created in Excel 2007–2016 have a .xlsx extension.

Hot Tip

The reason there are different file extensions for the different versions is because some of the features available in later versions of Excel are not applicable to earlier versions.

CLOSING EXCEL FILES WITHOUT CLOSING EXCEL

When closing down a file, you may not always want to quit out of the Excel program altogether. There are two ways to close files without closing Excel.

- ➔ **File menu/tab:** Click on the File menu, Office button or ribbon tab and select Close.

- ➔ **X-button:** If there are two x-shaped buttons at the top right corner of the Excel screen, click on the lower button to close the file (the upper button closes Excel). If there is only one x-shaped button, clicking on this will close Excel.

Hot Tip

If you have several files open in Excel (pre-2007) and want to close them all without closing Excel, hold down the Shift key on the keyboard, then click on the File menu and choose Close All.

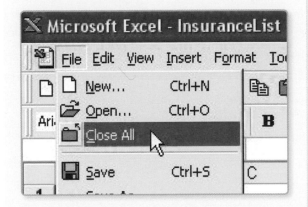

Above: Multiple files can be closed in pre-2007 versions of Excel by holding down the Shift key to open the file menu.

CRASH RECOVERY

If Excel develops a problem, a warning box will usually appear before the program closes. After closing down, Excel may automatically reopen – although in earlier versions you may need to re-open it manually. The files you were working on will reappear as recovered files. You will then have the opportunity to resave them without losing any changes.

Modifying Auto Recovery (2000-2003)

Excel recovers files by regularly saving them automatically. The frequency with which the auto-save function works can be modified if required, as long as you are using a version of Excel from 2000 onwards. In Excel 2000–2003, click on the Tools menu and choose Options. From the dialogue box that appears, select the Save tab and look for the words 'Save AutoRecover info every:' You can adjust the number next to this to indicate the frequency (in minutes) with which the files are saved.

Modifying Auto Recovery (2007-2016)

In Excel 2007, click on the Office button in the top left corner of the screen and choose Excel Options. In Excel 2010 and later versions, click on the File ribbon tab and choose Options. In both cases a dialogue box will appear. Choose Save from the list on the left and look for the AutoRecover information, where the value in minutes can be changed.

Above: You can change the frequency at which files are automatically saved.

MOVING AROUND EXCEL

Moving to specific cells to read information or enter data can result in lots of time wasted flicking the scroll wheel of the mouse or clicking on the scroll bar buttons. Fortunately, there are several other ways of quickly accessing a particular cell.

MOVING TO CELLS USING THE KEYBOARD

Understanding the keyboard shortcuts for moving around a spreadsheet can save a great deal of time. Below are some of the quickest ways of moving to particular cells.

Arrow Keys

The arrow keys on the keyboard are ideal for jumping from one cell to another. They are usually situated to the left of the number pad on the far right of the keyboard. On keyboards without a number pad (often on laptops), the arrow keys are usually near the bottom right corner.

Ctrl + Arrow Keys

Make sure a cell is selected inside a spreadsheet with a list of data below it. Hold down the Ctrl key on the keyboard (near the bottom left corner of the keyboard) and press the down arrow. The cell selector will jump down the screen to the next entry in that column followed by an empty cell.

Hot Tip

Press the End key once, then an arrow key to jump back to the first row or column, or down or across to the end of a section of data. The End key is indicated with a diagonal downwards arrow.

Keep on Jumping

Hold the Ctrl key and press the down arrow again to jump further down the list until you get to the very bottom of the spreadsheet. You can use the up, left and right arrow keys to move up and across a list in your spreadsheet in the same way.

Get Me Back!

If you need to get back to cell A1 in the top left corner of a spreadsheet, hold down the Ctrl key on the keyboard and press the Home key (marked with an upward-facing diagonal arrow). The cell selector will jump to cell A1. Similarly, press the Home key on its own to return to column A of the row in which the cell selector is positioned.

Find the End

The bottom right-hand corner of data entered into a spreadsheet can be selected by holding down the Ctrl key on the keyboard and pressing the End key. The cell selector may jump to an empty cell if data had previously been entered there but subsequently deleted. However, this is useful for quickly moving down and across to the bottom of a spreadsheet.

Above: The Go To dialogue box can be quickly opened by pressing the F5 key on the keyboard.

Go to a Cell

If you want to go to a specific cell and you know its reference, then press F5 on the keyboard. A Go To dialogue box will appear where a cell reference (e.g. H56) can be entered before clicking on OK. If you frequently use the Go To dialogue box, a list of cell references will appear, from which you can select the cell you want.

MOUSE SCROLLING

If your mouse has a scroll wheel, you can use this to scroll up and down your spreadsheet vertically (although it may not work for horizontal scrolling – if you only have a vertical scroll wheel, clicking the scroll wheel will activate horizontal and vertical scrolling). However, there is another use for most scroll wheels. Try clicking with it as though you are clicking the buttons on the mouse. If the mouse pointer on screen changes to a dot with four triangles, you can then scroll by simply moving the mouse in the direction you want to go. The further you move away from the centre of the screen, the faster it scrolls.

Above: Press the mouse's scroll wheel and the mouse pointer will change, allowing faster and easier scrolling around a spreadsheet.

Stop Scrolling

When you have reached the cell you require using the mouse's scroll wheel, return the pointer to the middle of the screen and click the scroll wheel again to switch off the mouse scroll function.

Hot Tip

Press Escape on the keyboard to stop automatically scrolling after clicking the mouse's scroll wheel.

SCROLL BARS

Excel spreadsheets each have two scroll bars – one for scrolling up and down, which is displayed down the right-hand side of the screen, and one for scrolling across, near the bottom right of the screen. Traditionally you can scroll up and down or across a spreadsheet by clicking on the triangles or arrows at the ends of the scroll bars, but there are much easier and faster ways of moving around a spreadsheet using the scroll bars.

Jumping a Page at a Time

If you need to scroll down or across a spreadsheet a page at a time, then position the mouse pointer inside the scroll bar, but not on the scroll-bar marker (the square or rectangle inside the scroll bar). Click on the left button and you will move up, down or across the screen a page at a time.

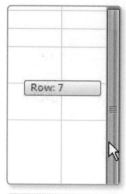

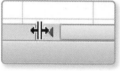

Above: The horizontal scroll bar can be widened using the control to its left.

Left: Dragging the scroll-bar marker provides fast scrolling, and an indicator of where you are scrolling to will appear on screen.

Dragging the Scroll-Bar Marker

Position the mouse pointer over the scroll-bar marker and hold down the left button. Move along the scroll bar to drag the marker and move up, down or across the spreadsheet. As you do this, a small message will appear displaying the row number or column letter you are scrolling to.

Resizing the Horizontal Scroll Bar

The width of the horizontal scroll bar can be altered by positioning the mouse to the left of the 'scroll left' triangle/ arrow. When the mouse pointer changes to a double-headed arrow with two lines through the middle, hold the left button down and drag this mouse pointer to alter the width of the horizontal scroll bar. Move left to make it wider and right to make it narrower.

SPLITTING SCREENS

If you need to view data that appears at the top and bottom of a worksheet at the same time, you can split the screen to show more than one view.

View-Split

Click on the View menu or ribbon tab and select Split. The screen will be split vertically and horizontally, allowing you to scroll through two separate views of the worksheet.

The split can be adjusted by hovering the mouse pointer over the horizontal or vertical split lines. When the mouse pointer changes to a double-headed arrow with two lines running through it, hold the left button down and drag the mouse pointer to adjust the split. To switch off the split, click on Split on the View menu or ribbon tab.

Left: In Excel 2010 and earlier versions, a worksheet can be split horizontally and vertically from the scroll bar.

Dragging the Split (Excel up to 2010)

Position the mouse pointer to the right of the triangle/arrow pointing right on the horizontal scroll bar, or above the triangle/arrow pointing upwards at the top of the vertical scroll bar. When the pointer changes to a double-headed arrow with two lines running through it, hold down the left button and drag the mouse pointer into the worksheet to split it. Release the left button on the mouse to set the split. You can now scroll through two separate views of the same worksheet. To switch off this split, hover the mouse over the split line. When the mouse pointer changes, drag the split line back to the top or side of the screen.

MOVING BETWEEN WORKSHEETS

If you have a lot of data in a spreadsheet, it can be helpful to spread it across a few worksheets (pages). Moving between these can be time consuming, so here are a couple of shortcuts.

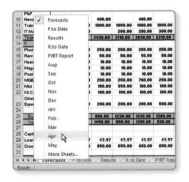

→ **Right-click:** If you have lots of sheet tabs, you may have to click on the scroll buttons near the bottom left corner of the screen to find them. However, there is a quicker way. Right-click on these scroll buttons and a list of all the sheet tabs will appear. Select one from the list and it will be opened instantly.

Above: Right-clicking on the sheet tab scroll buttons displays a checklist of sheets.

→ **Ctrl+Page Up/Down:** Hold down the Ctrl key on the keyboard, then press the Page Up and Page Down keys on the keyboard (usually found next to the Home and End keys) to move up and down the sheet tabs.

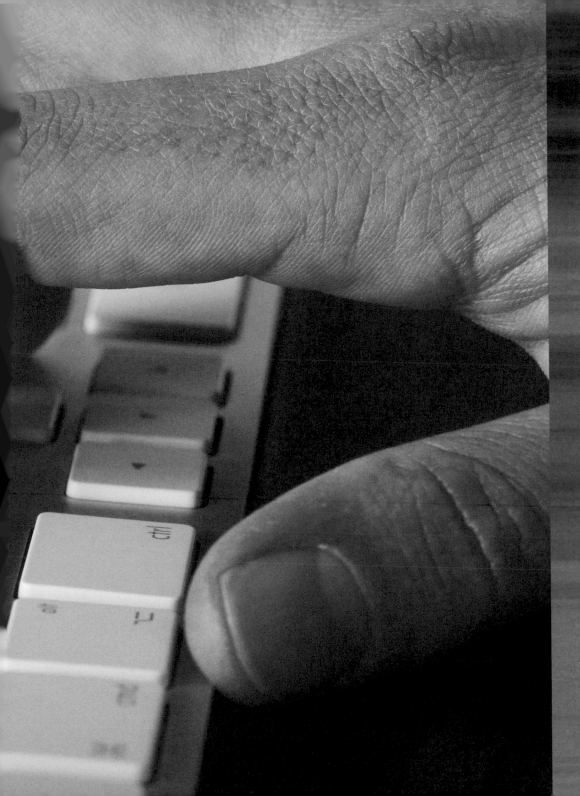

BASIC DATA MANIPULATION

BASIC RULES OF DATA ENTRY

Entering data into an Excel spreadsheet may seem straightforward, but there are some rules to adhere to, not to mention common mistakes to be aware of. One of the most important elements of basic entry is making sure that Excel knows when you have completed inputting data into a cell.

PRESS ENTER

When typing data into a cell, try to get into the habit of pressing Enter/Return on the keyboard when you have finished entering the information rather than just moving on to the next cell. Simply selecting another cell with the mouse or keyboard can lead to mistakes, especially if you are writing or editing a calculation.

Above: When entering data into a cell, a cross and a tick mark appear in the formula bar above the column headings.

Tick and Cross

When you begin to type words or numbers into a cell, a tick and a cross appear above the column headings (the letters across the top of the spreadsheet) in an area called the formula bar. In Excel 2003 and earlier versions, the tick mark is coloured green and the cross is coloured red (they are not coloured in Excel 2007–2016). These symbols only appear when you are entering data or editing the contents of a cell, and they indicate that some features in Excel are disabled.

The tick and the cross can be used to either confirm that an action has been completed or when you return to a cell to edit its contents in the following ways:

➔ **Click on the tick**: When entering data or editing the contents of a cell, you can click on the tick in the formula bar to confirm completion. This is an alternative method to pressing the Enter/Return key on the keyboard.

➔ **Cross it off**: If you are editing a cell and decide you want to revert to its original contents, click on the cross mark in the formula bar. This is similar to using the Undo button and will undo your last editing action.

Hot Tip

Press Escape on the keyboard to cancel editing a cell or entering data into it.

Above: When creating calculations, don't click in another cell to complete it, because the calculation will change – always press Enter or click on the tick mark.

DATA ENTRY SHORTCUTS

Entering data can become a mind- (and finger-) numbing task, especially if you have long lists of figures to input, but Excel offers a number of shortcuts and quick techniques to help speed up the process.

AUTOCOMPLETE

Excel automatically helps with entering data in a list format. It looks at the cells above the active cell and assumes that entries will be repeated. So, if you are inputting a list of household expenses, in which the words 'supermarket' and 'petrol' are repeated, you won't have to type them out in full every time. Excel will predict what you're typing based on the first letter or few letters, and you can press Enter on the keyboard to accept it.

Understanding AutoComplete

→ **Entries starting with the same letter**: If two or more entries in a list start with the same letter (e.g. 'gas bill' and 'groceries'), then Excel will wait for more letters to be entered before activating AutoComplete. For example, when typing the letters 'gr' Excel will display the word 'groceries'.

→ **Continuous list**: Excel only checks a continuous list of entries above a selected cell, so if there are any blank cells in a list, it will not check the entries above it.

→ **Capital letters**: If a word in a list begins with a capital letter, you do not need to start typing with

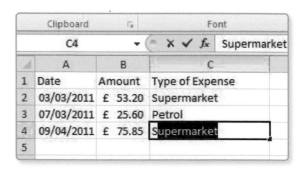

Above: Excel offers suggestions when entering data in a list, based on the entries above the selected cell.

a capital letter for AutoComplete to work. Excel will automatically follow the previous formatting of a word.

ALT+DOWN

AutoComplete is useful for speeding up input of list entries, but Excel offers another helpful feature that is ideal for long lists. To use this, select a cell at the bottom of a list, then hold down the Alt key on the keyboard and press the down arrow. A list of entries will appear, based on the contents of the cells above the one selected. Use the mouse to scroll up and down the list if it is too long to display all the entries in one window, and select an entry by left-clicking on it.

96	Feb-17	Food	92.05
97	Apr-17	Food	97.72
98	Apr-17	Food	98.34
99	May-17	Food	98.97
100	Jun-17	Food	123.30
101	Jun-17		
102		Food	
103		Mortgage	
		Petrol	
104		Utility bill	

Above: When entering data in a list, hold down the Alt key on the keyboard and press the down arrow on the keyboard to reveal a list of entries based on the contents of the cells above the selected cell.

Uses for Alt+Down

Using the Alt and down arrow keys on the keyboard to activate a list is not as quick as using AutoComplete, but it is a useful way of checking for mistakes in a list. It also ensures continuity and reduces the risk of errors in entering the same type of listing with different spellings.

AUTOFILL

When a block of cells needs to contain the same data, or a sequence of data (such as the names of days or months), you do not need to enter this information separately. The AutoFill feature in Excel does this for you. This can be quickly used when the mouse pointer is positioned in the bottom right corner of a selected cell, where the pointer changes to a black cross.

AutoFill Months or Days

To enter the months of the year (or days of the week) into a spreadsheet using AutoFill:

→ **Enter the first month in a cell and press Enter on the keyboard**

→ **Select the cell and hover the mouse over the bottom right corner of that cell**

→ **When the mouse pointer changes to a black cross, hold the left button down on the mouse and move up, down or across the screen to create a sequence of months**

→ **Release the left button on the mouse to enter the sequence**

Above: Creating a sequence of months involves entering only one month and using Excel's AutoFill feature. This can save hours of data entry.

Copying with AutoFill

Calculations, titles and numbers can all be quickly copied up, down or across a spreadsheet using AutoFill. Just select the cell you want to copy and hover the mouse pointer in the bottom right corner of the cell. When the mouse

Hot Tip

AutoFill is useful for creating a sequence of names with numbers. For example, if you need a list of weeks starting at Week 1, Week 2, Week 3, just enter Week 1 in a cell and use AutoFill to complete the sequence.

pointer changes to a black cross, hold down the left button on the mouse and move up, down or across the spreadsheet to start copying. Release the left button to stop copying.

AutoFill Number Sequences

If you require a specific sequence of numbers or dates, Excel needs to know what that sequence is. So, for a sequence of numbers such as 100, 200, 300, the first two numbers have to be entered in two adjacent cells. Next, these two cells have to be selected together (make sure the mouse pointer is a white cross and then swipe across them with the left button held down). Finally, position the mouse pointer at the bottom right corner of the selected cells and make sure it changes to a black cross before starting to AutoFill.

Hot Tip

If the cells to be copied into using AutoFill are in a table of data, try double clicking instead of dragging the AutoFill cross. Excel will automatically AutoFill the cells.

Above: Creating a sequence of numbers or dates using AutoFill requires data to be entered into two adjacent cells to show Excel the pattern of the sequence.

AutoFill Smart Tags

After using Excel's AutoFill feature to copy data or create a sequence, a small Smart Tag will appear at the bottom of the range of cells. Click on the Smart Tag to open a menu offering more AutoFill options, including Copy Cells, Fill Formatting and Fill Series. Smart Tags were introduced in Excel 2002 and can be found in all versions since then.

Left: After using the AutoFill feature in Excel 2002 or later versions, a Smart Tag appears to offer further copy options.

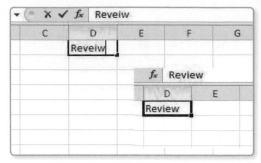

Above: Common spelling mistakes in Excel are automatically corrected after typing a word and pressing the space bar or the Enter/Return key.

AUTOCORRECT

Excel helps with spelling mistakes, repeated words and incorrect capital letters through its AutoCorrect feature. For example, if you type the word 'Reveiw', Excel will automatically correct this to 'Review' when you press the Enter/Return key. It will also correct the spelling after pressing the space bar if you wish to type more than word into a cell.

Avoiding AutoCorrect

If a word is automatically corrected by Excel, but you want it to remain as you had typed it, the quickest solution is to double click inside the cell in question to begin editing it, then correct the spelling and press Return/Enter. Excel will then bypass the automatic correction.

CAPITAL LETTER MISTAKES

Excel's AutoCorrect can automatically amend words where the CAPS lock has been left on or the Shift key has been pressed down for too long, resulting in the first two letters of a word being written in capitals.

Above: Accidentally leave the CAPS lock switched on and typed words may look like this, but Excel will automatically swap round the upper and lower case.

Forgotten to Switch off CAPS Lock?

If the CAPS lock is accidentally left switched on and all the letters typed are in capitals, Excel will automatically correct this. For example, if a word should be typed with an initial capital, such as 'Birmingham', leaving the CAPS lock on will result in 'bIRMINGHAM' (holding down the Shift key to type a capital when the CAPS lock is on reverts to a lower-case letter). Excel will automatically swap round the upper- and lower-case letters and switch off the CAPS lock.

CUSTOMIZING AUTOCORRECT

A number of settings within Excel's AutoCorrect can be customized and switched on or off. All these settings are displayed in an AutoCorrect dialogue box, which can be opened in pre-2007 versions of Excel by clicking on the Tools menu and choosing AutoCorrect. In Excel 2007, click on the multicoloured Office button at the top left of the screen, and in Excel 2010–16, click on the File menu ribbon tab. In both cases a menu appears, from which you can select Options or Excel Options. From the dialogue box, choose Proofing from the list on the left and click on the AutoCorrect Options button in the main part of the dialogue box.

Hot Tip

In Excel 2002 and 2003, when a spelling mistake or misuse of capital letters is AutoCorrected, click on its Smart Tag for a list of options for reversing the correction or switching off the function completely.

Capital Corrections and Exceptions

The AutoCorrect dialogue box has a tick box list of capital letter-related corrections that can be switched on or off. Adjusting these can help avoid the problems of typing with the CAPS lock accidentally switched on, or typing two capital letters at the start of a word.

Left: The AutoCorrect dialogue box has a tick list of capital letter corrections, which are useful for reducing the risk of typing errors.

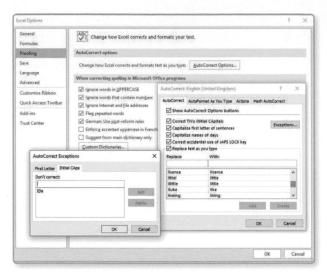

Above: Words and abbreviations that need two capital letters at the beginning can be added to an Exceptions list in AutoCorrect.

AutoCorrect Exceptions

Sometimes words or abbreviations do actually require two capital letters at the beginning (e.g. IDs), or perhaps you want a word to begin with a lower case followed by upper-case letters. These can be added to an Exceptions list. In the AutoCorrect dialogue box, click on the Exceptions button and another dialogue box will appear where such entries can be added.

SPELLING CORRECTIONS

A list of words that will be automatically corrected can be found, alphabetically organized, in the lower half of the AutoCorrect dialogue box. This lists common spelling and typographical errors. The top half of this list comprises AutoCorrect entries for inserting copyright and trademark symbols, etc.

Removing AutoCorrect Spelling Corrections

If you want to remove an AutoCorrect spelling correction, select it from the list in the AutoCorrect

Hot Tip

When holding down the Shift key on the keyboard to type a capital letter, it's all too easy to type the second letter in capitals if you do not release the Shift key fast enough. Excel will automatically correct this mistake, leaving only one capital letter at the beginning of the word.

dialogue box, then click on the Delete button. If you accidentally delete the wrong one, click on the Add button immediately and it will be re-entered.

Adding Your Own AutoCorrections

You can customize the AutoCorrect list by adding your own frequently mistyped words. In the AutoCorrect dialogue box, enter the incorrect version of a word in the left box, beneath Replace. Enter the correct spelling in the right box, beneath With. Click on the Add button and your entry will be listed.

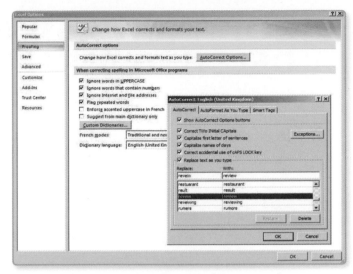

Above: Excel has a list of typical spelling mistakes and corrections, but you can add your own common mistakes to this list.

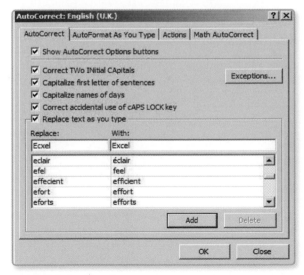

Above: You can add your own frequent misspellings to Excel's AutoCorrect function.

COPYING, PASTING, MOVING, DELETING AND EDITING

Copying and rearranging existing data can save hours of repetitive typing. Excel offers a variety of options for copying and moving data, along with a number of time-saving shortcuts.

SELECTING CELLS

One of the most awkward and frustrating aspects of cutting and copying cells is selecting them quickly and easily. You might find that you select too many cells, lose the selected cells or even move them to the wrong location. Below are some of the most common methods of selecting and moving cells within a worksheet.

	A
2	Monday
3	Tuesday
4	Wednesday
5	Thursday
6	Friday

Above: When swiping over and selecting cells using the mouse with the left button held down, always make sure the mouse pointer is a large white cross before starting.

Swipe with the Mouse
The most popular method of selecting a block of cells is to swipe over them while holding down the left button of the mouse. However, this can go wrong if the mouse pointer is not showing as a large white cross to start with, so always make sure the pointer is set correctly before you start.

Shift and Arrow Keys
While the arrow keys on the keyboard allow the cell selector to move around the grid of a spreadsheet, you can press the Shift key to select the cells to which the cell selector moves instead.

Ctrl, Shift and Arrow Keys
Using the Ctrl, Shift and arrow keys is ideal for selecting a large list of data.

- ⮕ **Select one cell in the top left corner of the list**
- ⮕ **Hold down the Ctrl and Shift keys**
- ⮕ **Press the down arrow once**

Hot Tip

If you want to select across rather than down a list, use the same instructions as above but use the right arrow instead of the down arrow.

The cell selector will jump to the bottom of the list or to the point where the first empty space exists (repeat this process if you need to move further down). All the cells from the top corner of the list to this first empty cell will be selected.

Ctrl, Shift and Space Bar

An entire list or table of data can be instantly selected by going to one cell inside the list, then holding down the Ctrl and Shift keys and pressing the space bar once. Note, however, that if there are blank rows or columns of cells in a table or list, Excel may not select the entire range of data.

Hot Tip

Tidy up your data before selecting it by deleting unwanted rows or columns.

Above: The Shift and click method is one of the quickest ways of selecting a large group of cells.

Shift and Click

The Shift and click method is one of the easiest and safest ways of highlighting a range of cells. It works by selecting opposite corners of this range, so if a table or list has to be selected, first click on the cell in the top left corner, for example, then scroll down to the opposite bottom right corner. Position the mouse pointer over that cell, hold down the Shift key and left-click once with the mouse. Note that this only works if you hold down the Shift key before clicking with the mouse.

Ctrl and Click

Similar to the Shift and click technique is to hold down the Ctrl key on the keyboard and left-click inside different cells. As long as the Ctrl key remains pressed, all the cells you click on will be selected. You can even swipe over a range of cells by holding down the left button and moving across them.

CUT, COPY AND PASTE TECHNIQUES

Cut, copy and paste are some of the traditional computer terms that allow information to be removed, duplicated and moved. Over the years, various shortcuts for using them have evolved.

Keyboard Shortcuts

➔ **Cut:** Hold down the Ctrl key on the keyboard and press X. A moving dotted line will appear around the selected cell or cells. Select another cell and press Return/Enter to instantly cut and paste the cell(s) to the new destination.

➔ **Copy:** Hold down the Ctrl key and press C on the keyboard. Excel will add a moving dotted line around the selected cell or cells. Select another cell and press Return/Enter to paste the cell(s) to the new destination instantly.

Hot Tip

When a cell, or range of cells, is cut or copied in Excel, moving dotted lines appear around the cell(s). These can be removed by pressing Escape on the keyboard. This also cancels the cut/copy instruction.

Paste: Once a cell, range of cells or another piece of data has been cut or copied, select the destination cell (or the first cell in a range), hold down the Ctrl key on the keyboard and press V.

Right-Click Shortcuts

After selecting a cell or range of cells to be cut or copied, right-click inside them and choose Cut or Copy from the menu that appears. Right-click in the cell where the cut or copied data is going to, then choose Paste from the menu that appears.

Edit Menu (pre-2007)

The Edit menu in pre-2007 versions of Excel lists the options to Cut, Copy and Paste. Once a cell or range of cells has been selected, click on this menu to cut or copy, then select a destination cell before returning to the menu and choosing to reinsert the data.

Hot Tip

A cell or range of cells can be moved by selecting them, then pressing Shift and Delete on the keyboard. Move to a destination cell and press Enter/Return to move them.

	A	B	C
2	01/01/2011	ARMACY	£10.07
3	03/01/2011	E 2814	£8.46
4	05/01/2011	E 2814	£5.00
5	07/01/2011	TORY SHOP	£16.00
6	09/01/2011		£23.96
7	11/01/2011	S S/MKT	£69.50
8	13/01/2011	E 2808	£7.97
9	15/01/2011	DIRECT DEBIT PAYMENT - TH	-£578.62

Above: One of the quickest methods of cutting, copying and pasting is to right click with the mouse and choose the respective options from the menu.

Hot Tip

After cutting or copying a cell or range of cells in Excel, the fastest way to paste them is to select a destination cell and press Enter/Return on the keyboard.

Toolbar Buttons

The Cut, Copy and Paste toolbar buttons have become an instantly recognizable set of symbols in Excel and most other computer programs. In pre-2007 versions of Excel they are displayed on the Standard toolbar. In Excel 2007–2016 they are displayed in the top left corner of the screen when the Home ribbon tab is selected.

PASTE SMART TAGS (EXCEL 2002-2016)

When a cell, a range of cells or other data is pasted into Excel, the pasted cell or cells have a Smart Tag in the bottom right corner. This Smart Tag provides a drop-down menu (just click on it to open the menu), with a variety of options to help with pasting. It can also help with issues such as narrow column widths or incorrect formatting. In Excel 2016, the Smart Tag provides options for Conditional Formatting and inserting Charts (depending on what has been copied).

> ## Hot Tip
>
> If you want to copy the contents of a cell to the cell below it, just select the empty cell below, hold down the Ctrl key on the keyboard and press D to paste in the contents from above.

	A	B	C	D	E
1	01/01/2011	LLOYDS PH	£10.07		
2	03/01/2011	TESCO STC	£8.46		
3	05/01/2011	TESCO STC	£5.00		
4	07/01/2011	CLARKS FA	£16.00		
5	09/01/2011	GAP 7982	£23.96		
6	11/01/2011	SAINSBUR	£69.50		
7	13/01/2011	TESCO STC	£7.97		
8	15/01/2011	DIRECT DE	-£578.62		
9					

Above: After pasting in Excel versions 2002–2016 a Smart Tag appears containing a number of efficient pasting options.

MULTIPLE COPYING WITH THE CLIPBOARD

When Excel 2002 was released, it included a Clipboard that could be used across the entire Office 2002 suite of programs (including Outlook, Word and PowerPoint). This allowed up to 24 items to be copied and listed on the Clipboard, then pasted in turn into different programs.

Using the Clipboard (2002 and 2003)

The Clipboard is displayed down the right side of the screen and can be opened by clicking on the Edit menu and choosing Office Clipboard. When a cell or range of cells is copied, they are listed in the Clipboard with the most recent at the top. To paste an item from the Clipboard into Excel, select the appropriate cell, then click on the item listed in the Clipboard.

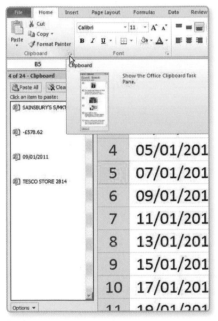

Above: The Clipboard in Excel versions 2007–2016 is displayed down the left side of the screen and activated via the Clipboard option on the Home ribbon.

Using the Clipboard (2007-2016)

The Clipboard is displayed down the left side of the screen and can be opened by selecting the Home ribbon tab and clicking on Clipboard near the top left of the screen (or the arrow marker to the right of it). When a cell or range of cells is copied, they are listed in the Clipboard with the most recent at the top. To paste an item from the Clipboard into Excel, select the appropriate cell, then click on the item listed in the Clipboard.

Removing Items from the Clipboard

To clear items from the Clipboard, hover the mouse pointer over one of the copied items listed. A box will appear around it with a drop-down triangle to the right. Click on this triangle and a short menu will appear with the option to delete the entry. Click on Delete to remove the item from the Clipboard.

PASTE SPECIAL

Paste Special is one of the more traditional features of Excel. It can be useful for copying data from another program and choosing how to paste it into a spreadsheet. A Paste Special dialogue box is used to instruct Excel on how the data should be pasted. Depending on the version of Excel, this dialogue box can be opened (once data has been cut or copied) by right-clicking inside a cell and choosing Paste Special, or by clicking on the Edit menu in early versions of Excel and choosing Paste Special. The following list outlines some of the options in this dialogue box.

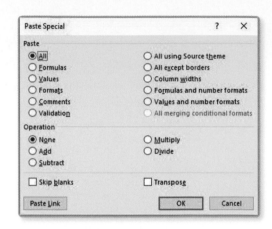

Above: The Paste Special dialogue box is a traditional way of customizing how data is pasted into Excel before being added to the spreadsheet.

➔ **Values:** This is useful for copying cells containing calculations and formulae that may not render correctly if being pasted from a different spreadsheet. By pasting values, only the results of the calculations at the time of copying are pasted.

➔ **Formats:** This pastes only the formatting of the copied cell(s), leaving the contents unchanged. It can be useful for copy-pasting the presentation of cells without changing any values.

➔ **Column Widths:** This option only pastes the width of the columns from the copied cell(s). This can help if column widths need to be a standard size.

➔ **Add/Subtract/Multiply/Divide:** These options will calculate the copied cells with the pasted cells (values are needed in both). It is a useful function for updating figures by adding new ones to existing data.

➔ **Skip Blanks:** This can be used when updating weekly or monthly results where, if there is a blank cell in the copied data, it will not create a blank cell in the pasted data. Instead, the original value will remain. Note that this only works when pasting over existing data.

> ## Hot Tip
> The Multiply option is also handy for calculating percentages of figures.

➔ **Transpose:** If data is displayed the wrong way round (down the screen instead of across it, for example), then Transpose is a lifeline. As long as there is enough space in the spreadsheet, Excel will switch the cells listed down the spreadsheet to display them across it, or vice versa.

➔ **Paste Link:** In this function, the original copied cells are linked to the pasted cells, so when their values change, the pasted cells also change. This is very useful for summarizing results on one page and making sure they are always up to date.

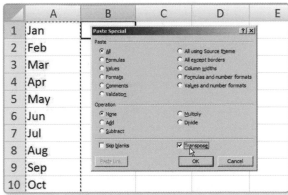

Above: If a range of cells is displayed down the screen but you want them to run across it, use Paste Special's Transpose feature to rearrange them.

DELETING DATA

There are several ways of deleting cells, and the method you choose should be guided by what it is that needs deleting.

Deleting Cell Contents

The quickest way of deleting the contents of a cell or range of cells is to select the cell(s) and press Delete on the keyboard. This will only delete the data in the cells, though – it will not remove any formatting.

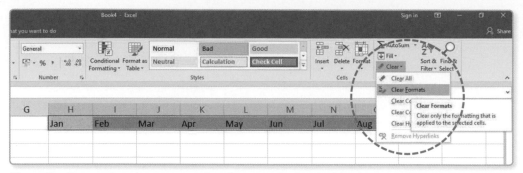

Above: Clear Formats allows the appearance of a cell or range of cells to be deleted without deleting the data in them.

Hot Tip

Don't use the space bar to delete cells. This overwrites the cell with a space and removes the contents, but it leaves unwanted spaces within the cell.

Deleting Cell Formatting (pre-2007)

The colours, borders and other formatting used in a cell or range of cells can be removed without deleting the contents. Once the cell or cells are selected, click on the Edit menu and choose Clear. From the sub-menu that appears, select Formats.

Deleting Cell Formatting (2007-2016)

To remove cell formatting in later versions of Excel, select the relevant cell or cells, make sure the Home ribbon tab is selected and look at the top right corner of the screen for a Clear option. Click on the drop-down triangle for this and a menu will appear. Select Clear Formats.

	A	B	C
2	01/01/2011	LLOYDS PHARMACY	£10.07
3	03/01/2011	TESCO STORE 2814	£8.46
4	05/01/2011	TESCO STORE 2814	£5.00
5	/2011	CLARKS FACTORY SHOP	£16.00
6	/2011	SAINSBURY'S S/MKT	£69.50
7	/2011	TESCO STORE 2808	£7.97
8	/2011	DIRECT DEBIT PAYMENT - TH	-£578.62
9	/2011	ASDA STORES/PETROL/	£60.23

Above: Right-clicking on a row number or column letter will allow you to delete the whole section.

Deleting Rows and Columns

You can quickly delete an entire row or column from a spreadsheet by right-clicking on the row number or column letter and choosing Delete from the menu that appears.

EDITING DATA

If you need to edit or amend the contents of a cell or several cells, use one of the following shortcuts.

➔ **Press F2**: Select the cell to edit, then press F2 on the keyboard. A flashing cursor will appear inside the selected cell and its contents can be edited using the arrow keys, delete and backspace.

→ **Double-click:** Position the mouse pointer inside the cell that needs to be edited, then double-click with the left mouse button. A flashing cursor will appear where the mouse pointer was positioned.

Hot Tip

When editing the contents of a cell, press the Home key on the keyboard to jump to the start of it and the End key to jump to the end of the line.

→ **Formula bar:** Select the cell to be edited. Its contents will be displayed in the formula bar, above the column letter headings. Move the mouse pointer into the formula bar and over the contents of the cell. The mouse pointer will change to an I-beam. Click once with the left button to begin editing the cell.

Fast Editing with Find and Replace

If you want to replace every instance of a particular word in a spreadsheet, you can save hours of typing by using the Find and Replace feature.

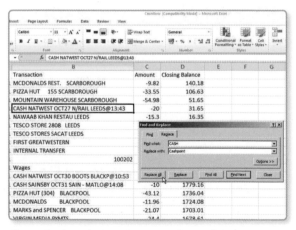

Above: Excel's Find and Replace is a quick way of changing a word or series of words within multiple cells.

→ **Hold down the Ctrl key and press the letter F**

→ **In the dialogue box, click on the Replace tab**

→ **Type the word you want to replace in the Find What section**

→ **Type the word you want to replace it with in the Replace With box**

→ **Click on Find Next to identify the words and then Replace to change them**

→ **If you're confident it works, just click on Replace All**

CHANGING ROWS AND COLUMNS

The width and height of columns and rows in a spreadsheet can be altered to accommodate text that doesn't fit within them. Additional rows and columns can be inserted or removed to add more data or remove unwanted sections.

CHANGING COLUMN WIDTH

If the width of a column is too wide – or not wide enough – there are a couple of easy ways to adjust it. Both techniques involve positioning the mouse pointer between the column letters and to the right of the column that needs to be widened or narrowed. The mouse pointer will change to a black cross with double horizontal arrows. Once the mouse pointer is this shape, do one of the following:

- **Double-click:** If you double-click with the left button on the mouse, the width of the column will automatically resize to the widest data in that column. If there is no data in the column, it will remain the same size.

- **Click and drag:** Hold down the left button and move it to the left to reduce the width of the column, or to the right to widen it.

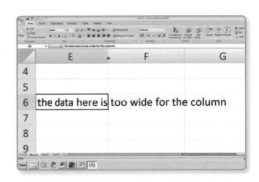

Above: To adjust the column width, start by positioning the mouse pointer between two column heading letters.

CHANGING ROW HEIGHT

Changing the height of a row uses the same basic techniques as altering the width of a column. Position the mouse pointer between two row numbers, and when it appears as a

Above: Selecting multiple rows or columns allows several of them to be resized at the same time.

black cross with double-headed vertical arrows, hold the left button down and drag the mouse pointer down the screen to increase the height of the row, or double-click to resize it automatically.

SELECTING MULTIPLE ROWS OR COLUMNS

Multiple rows can be resized at the same time, and so can multiple columns. However, you cannot resize both multiple rows and columns at the same time.

To select a block of rows or columns, swipe over the numbers or letters with the left mouse button held down. If the rows or columns you want to select are not grouped together (for example, if you want to select columns A, G and L), use the mouse to highlight the first column letter, hold down the Ctrl key on the keyboard and select the remaining column letters. The same process can be used with rows.

RESIZING MULTIPLE ROWS OR COLUMNS

Once a number of rows or columns have been selected, position the mouse pointer to the right of one of the selected column letters or below one of the selected row numbers. When the mouse pointer changes to a black cross with two arrows, double-click to automatically resize all the columns, or hold the left mouse button down and drag the mouse pointer to resize them all.

Hot Tip

Select several rows or columns together by first selecting one with the mouse, then hold down the Shift key on the keyboard and use the arrow keys to select more rows or columns.

INSERTING ROWS AND COLUMNS

There are two quick methods for adding extra rows and columns within existing data in a spreadsheet.

Right Click

To insert a row, position the mouse pointer on the row number below where you want the new row to be added. To insert a column, position the mouse pointer over a column letter to the right of where an extra column needs to be inserted. In both cases, right click with the mouse and choose Insert from the menu that appears. An extra row or column will be added.

Above: An extra row can be quickly inserted by right-clicking on a row number and choosing Insert from the menu.

Ctrl and +

Select a row where an extra row needs to inserted above it, or select a column where an extra column needs to be inserted to the left of it (click on a row number or column letter to select that row or column). Hold down the Ctrl key on the keyboard, then press the + key. An extra row or column will be inserted. If this does not work, try holding down the Ctrl and Shift keys together, then press the + key on the keyboard.

Above: Rows and columns can be quickly removed by right-clicking on their numbers or letters and choosing Delete.

DELETING ROWS AND COLUMNS

Removing rows and columns is similar to inserting them. After right-clicking on a row number or column letter, choose Delete from the menu that appears. Alternatively, select a row or column, hold down the Ctrl key on the keyboard and press the − (minus) key to remove that row or column.

FORMATTING DATA

Presentation is important, especially when you need to ensure information such as up-to-the-minute sales results are highlighted and easily visible. Excel contains a number of formatting tools to emphasize information within your spreadsheets.

FORMATTING TOOLBAR BUTTONS

The toolbar in Excel can be used for all sorts of formatting, including changing the font and size, adding bold and altering cell, border and text colour. The toolbar buttons will probably be familiar from other computer programs; however, they do differ between earlier and more recent versions of Excel itself.

Hot Tip

Change a cell's contents to bold by selecting the cell, then holding down the Ctrl key on the keyboard and pressing the letter B. Repeat this to switch off bold.

Formatting Toolbar (pre-2007)

The formatting toolbar buttons (font, size, colour, bold) are all displayed on the Formatting toolbar. If no buttons are visible, right click on any toolbar button and a checklist of toolbars will appear. Tick the box against Formatting to make the buttons visible.

Left: The formatting toolbar buttons in Excel 2003 and earlier versions are displayed on the Formatting toolbar.

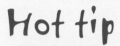

Hot tip

The font list is alphabetically sorted and the size list is numerically sorted.

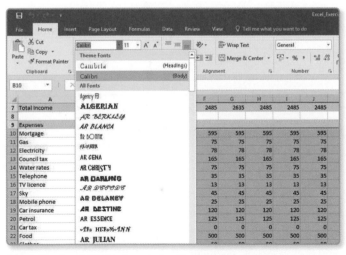

Formatting Toolbar (2007-2016)

In Excel 2007–2016, the most useful formatting

Above: The formatting toolbar buttons are found on the Home ribbon tab in Excel 2007–2016.

toolbar buttons can be found on the Home ribbon tab. Click on this near the top left corner of the screen and the formatting buttons will also be displayed there.

Above: The list of different fonts in Excel is displayed in alphabetical order with a sample of each one.

Changing the Font, Size and Colour of Text

The font, size and colour of data displayed in a spreadsheet can be quickly changed by selecting it (swipe over the cells with the left button held down on the mouse), then selecting the font, size and colour you want from the drop-down list in the toolbar menu.

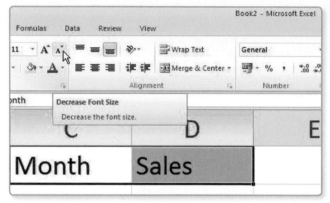

Above: The size of font used in a selected cell can be increased or reduced using the toolbar buttons on the Home ribbon tab.

Increasing and Decreasing Font Size (2007–2016)

The size of the font in a selected cell or group of cells can be increased or decreased using a couple of toolbar buttons from the Formatting toolbar on the Home ribbon tab. Both buttons have a capital letter A on them along with a triangle pointing up or down. The button with the larger letter A increases the font size; the button with the smaller letter A decreases the font size.

Fast Formatting (2007–2016)

When editing the contents of a cell, double-click on a word to select it and a small toolbar will appear next to the selected text. The toolbar will look slightly translucent but will change to full strength when the mouse pointer is positioned inside it. The buttons on this toolbar can be used to change the font, size, colour and other aspects of the selected text. A larger toolbar appears, along with a shortcut menu, when you right-click inside a cell.

FORMAT CELLS DIALOGUE BOX

The traditional method of changing the look of a cell or group of cells is to use the Format Cells dialogue box. This box can be opened by right-clicking inside a selected cell or group of cells and choosing Format Cells. The dialogue box contains a series of tabs to allow data to be set, for example, as currency, displayed vertically, wrapped inside a cell and re-coloured. The Format Cells function has many uses, the most useful of which are covered below.

Hot Tip

Quickly open the Format Cells dialogue box in Excel 2007–2016 by holding down the Ctrl and Shift keys on the keyboard, then pressing the letter F.

Setting Data to Currency

To set data to currency in the
Format Cells dialogue box:

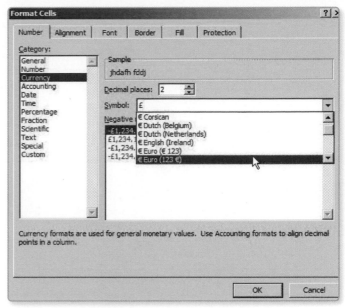

- Click on the Number tab
- Find and select Currency
- Choose the number of
  decimal places (e.g. 2 for
  amounts such as £1.50
  and £150.00)
- Select the currency symbol
- Choose a format for
  negative values (red and/
  or with a minus symbol)
- Click OK

Above: Data can be displayed with a currency symbol by selecting
it in the Format Cells dialogue box.

Setting a Percentage

When a calculation is created, such as
percentage mark-up, the result is not always displayed as a percentage, so it has to be changed.
Excel may have a % toolbar button to do this, but if it doesn't, take the following steps:

- Open the Format Cells
  dialogue box
- Click on the Number tab
- Select the Percentage option
  from the list on the left
- Choose the number of decimal
  places (e.g. 2 for percentages
  to read 2.00%)
- Click OK

Hot Tip

The pound sign (£) is usually
displayed as standard, but there
is a drop-down list where euros, dollars
and other currencies can
be selected.

Correcting a Date

Excel will usually display a date correctly when you enter it into a cell. However, if you find the date is being incorrectly rendered, open the Format Cells dialogue box and click on the Number tab. Select Date from the list on the left, then choose a suitable date Type from the list on the right. Click on OK to close the dialogue box.

Hot Tip

Excel sometimes becomes tangled up with percentages and displays them as 1 (a rounded-up whole number). If this happens, make sure the formatting of the cell is changed to percentage.

Date Problems

If a date is entered into a cell, Excel will automatically format that cell to display it as a date. However, if a number is later entered into the cell, it may be converted into a date because Excel uses a number system for date calculations. To fix this problem:

- ➔ **Select the cell in question**
- ➔ **Open the Format Cells dialogue box**
- ➔ **Click on the Number tab**
- ➔ **Select Number from the list on the left**
- ➔ **Choose the number of decimal places**
- ➔ **Click OK**

Angled Text and Numbers

Text or numbers inside a cell can be displayed at an angle to help squeeze it in and reduce the width of a table or list. To set the text at an angle:

- ➔ **Select the cells in which you want this format to be applied**
- ➔ **Open the Format Cells dialogue box**
- ➔ **Click on the Alignment tab**

- Go to the Orientation section in the top right corner
- Adjust the Degrees value or drag the orientation pointer to change the angle
- Click OK to see the results in the spreadsheet

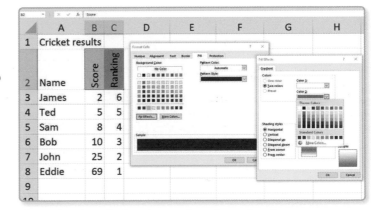

Above: The angle of text displayed in a cell can be changed via the Format Cells dialogue box and the Alignment tab.

Wrapping Text

If the text inside a cell stretches too far across the width of its column, but you don't want to widen the column, you can wrap the text so it displays across two or more lines within the cell. You may want to change the width of the column or height of the row. To instruct Excel to wrap the text:

- Select the cell in question
- Open the Format Cells dialogue box
- Click on the Alignment tab
- Add a tick mark against Wrap Text
- Click OK to see the results

Adding Fill

Excel has some fantastic cell-colouring options, which can transform the look of a

Above: The colour of cells can be given the professional touch using Fill Effects from the Format Cells dialogue box.

spreadsheet. To colour cells, select the ones you want to apply this formatting to, then open the Format Cells dialogue box and click on the Fill tab. A standard set of colours will be displayed, but click on the Fill Effects button below them. A Fill Effects dialogue box will appear with options to add two colours to a cell and a choice of shading. After making a choice, click OK in both dialogue boxes to see the results.

FAST FORMATTING WITH AUTOFORMAT

It's easy to spend hours changing the look of a table or list by adding new colours, resizing the text and changing the font type. However, Excel has a useful feature called AutoFormat, which can do all this instantly for a table or list.

AutoFormat (pre-2007)

Select one cell inside the list or table of data, then click on the Format menu and choose AutoFormat. A dialogue box will appear with a selection of pre-formatted tables. Select a table format from the list on the left and a sample will be displayed to the right. Click on OK to apply the formatting to the data in the spreadsheet.

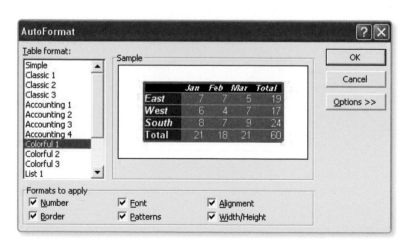

Above: The AutoFormat dialogue box in Excel 2003 and earlier versions provides a list of different styles and colours that can be applied to a table of data.

Table AutoFormat (2007–2016)

Select all the cells in a table that need to be formatted, then make sure the Home ribbon tab is visible. Find the Styles ribbon and a toolbar labelled Format as Table (on the right of the ribbon). Click on its drop-down triangle for a choice of table styles. Choose one and a small box will appear confirming the cells that will be formatted. Make sure the range of cells is correct, then click on OK. A series of drop-down triangles may be added to the table, along with a column or row number.

More Table AutoFormat (2007–2016)

After automatically formatting a table or list in Excel 2007–2016, a new ribbon called Table Tools Design will appear near the top middle of the screen. From here, a variety of modifications can be made. Within the table, a series of drop-down triangles can be triggered, providing additional menus that allow you to sort and filter data, for example.

COPYING FORMATTING

The colours, fonts and sizes used within a cell can be automatically applied to other cells so you don't have to format each one individually. There are a few methods of copying formatting.

Copy-Paste Smart Tag (2002–2013)

Copy a cell where the formatting needs to be used elsewhere,

Hot Tip

If you can't see the Table Tools Design ribbon in Excel 2007–2016 after formatting, make sure that one cell is selected inside the table.

Above: AutoFormat in Excel 2007–2016 provides an assortment of table colours, plus additional features such as sort and filter options.

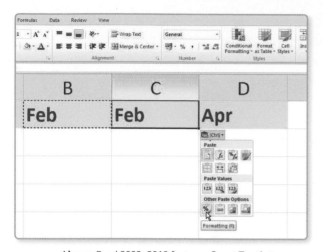

Above: Excel 2002–2013 feature a Smart Tag that appears after copy-pasting a cell, allowing the formatting to be copied without copying the contents.

then select the destination cell and choose Paste. The contents and the formatting of the cell will be copied and a Smart Tag will appear at the bottom right corner of the cell. Click on the Smart Tag and choose the Formatting option. The original contents of the cell will be displayed, but the formatting will have been copied across.

Copy Paste Special

Once you have copied a cell, you can apply the formatting to additional cells, too. Select the destination cells and either click on the Edit menu and choose Paste Special, or right-click inside the selected cell(s) and choose Paste Special. From the dialogue box that appears, select Formats and click OK. Only the formatting will be copied across into the destination cell(s).

Format Painter

The Format Painter toolbar button can be used for copying the format of a cell without copying the contents. In Excel 2007–2016, Format Painter can be found on the Clipboard ribbon in the top left corner of the screen, on the Home ribbon tab. In earlier versions of Excel, it is on the Standard toolbar, next to the Cut, Copy and Paste buttons.

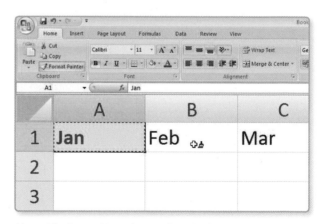

Above: The Format Painter button allows the formatting to be copied from one cell to multiple cells.

Copying Formats with Format Painter

Select a cell containing the formatting that needs to be copied. Click once on the Format Painter button and a series of flashing lines will appear around the selected cell. The mouse pointer will also have a Format Painter brush attached to it. Select the cell or group of cells to copy the formatting into. If you need to duplicate this several times, double click on the Format Painter button to switch it on permanently. Press Escape on the keyboard to switch it off, or click on the Format Painter toolbar button again.

REMOVING FORMATTING

One of the quickest methods of removing the formatting from a cell (or several cells) is to select it/them and use the Clear Formats option. In Excel 2003 and earlier versions this is available by clicking on the Edit menu, selecting Clear and choosing Formats from the sub-menu that appears.

In Excel 2007–2016, make sure the Home ribbon tab is selected, then look near the top right corner of the screen for the Editing ribbon and the word Clear with a drop-down triangle. Click on this and choose Clear Formats from the menu that appears.

Above: Clear Formats in Excel 2007–2016 is found on the Home ribbon tab. It removes the formatting of selected cells, but not the contents.

CHANGING DATA COLOUR

Data displayed in an Excel spreadsheet can change colour, depending on its value, by using a feature called Conditional Formatting. This can be useful for highlighting payments in on a bank statement or overdrawn closing balances. A list of unpaid invoices could highlight the invoice date when the difference between it and the current date becomes greater than 30 days.

STEP-BY-STEP: USING CONDITIONAL FORMATTING IN EXCEL 1997–2003

The following step-by-step guide shows how to set up a downloaded bank statement to display payments in (credits) with an easy-to-see colour and to highlight overdrawn closing balances in red.

1   Select the column where the value of each transaction is listed. In this example, there are minus values for payments out and positive values for payments in. To select an entire column, position the mouse pointer over the column heading letter and click once with the left button. The entire column will be selected.

2   Click on the Format menu and choose Conditional Formatting. A dialogue box will appear. Click on the second drop-down list from the left and choose the words 'Greater Than'. This

will make sure that any value that is greater than zero (a payment in) will be coloured and easy to see.

3 After choosing the Greater Than option, click inside the box to the right of this and type in the number 0. The condition has now been set that any cell greater than zero will be formatted. We now have to set up the formatting.

4 Click on the Format button inside the Conditional Formatting dialogue box. A second dialogue box will appear, from which the colour of the font can be changed, a cell border can be added and the cell can be filled with a colour. Choose some formatting options, then click on OK.

5 The formatting that has been chosen will be displayed in the Conditional Formatting dialogue box. Check the settings to make sure the criteria is set to any

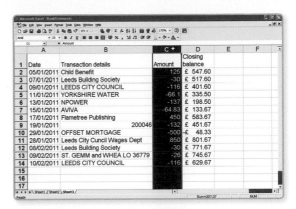

Above: Select a column of values to apply Conditional Formatting to and see them change colour.

Above: The Conditional Formatting dialogue box has a choice of formatting criteria; values can be greater than, less than, equal to and more.

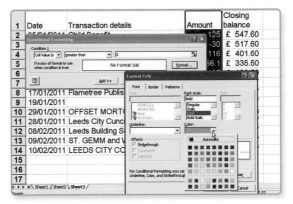

Above: Setting up the formatting to be applied with Conditional Formatting is quite restrictive – the colour of the font can be changed, but not the size or type of font, for example.

value that is greater than zero. If this is correct, click OK to see if any of the selected cells have changed (if there are any payments in).

6   The heading for the selected column will probably be coloured because Excel has calculated that it is greater than zero. To remove this formatting, select the cell in question, then click on the Edit menu, choose Clear and select Formats from the sub-menu.

7   Conditional Formatting can be useful for spotting overdrawn balances on bank statements. Select the closing balance column and reopen the Conditional Formatting dialogue box. Set the criteria to less than zero and set up some formatting, such as colouring the type red.

STEP-BY-STEP: USING CONDITIONAL FORMATTING IN EXCEL 2007-2016

The following step-by-step guide shows how to set up a downloaded bank statement to display payments in (credits) with an easy-to-see colour and highlight overdrawn closing balances in red.

1   Select the column where the value of each transaction is listed. In this example, there are minus values for payments out and positive values for payments in. To select an entire column, position the mouse pointer over the column heading letter and click once with the left button. The entire column will be selected.

2   Make sure the Home ribbon tab is selected, then look at the Styles ribbon near the top of the screen. One of the buttons on this ribbon should be Conditional Formatting. Click on it to activate a drop-down menu.

3   In the drop-down menu, select Highlight Cells Rules and choose Greater Than from the sub-menu. A small box will now appear on the screen.

4   With the Greater Than box displayed on screen, change the value in the first box (left side)

to the number 0. Next, click on the drop-down list for the right box and choose a colouring to apply to any values that are more than zero (payments in).

5 After selecting this colour, the formatting will be instantly applied on screen. Click on OK to close the Greater Than box and return to the spreadsheet.

6 The heading for the selected column will probably be coloured because Excel has calculated it is greater than zero. To remove this formatting, select the cell, then click on the Clear button at the top right of the screen and choose Clear Formats from the menu that appears.

7 Conditional Formatting can also be applied to the closing balance column to colour cells that are less than zero, indicating an overdrawn balance. To do this, repeat steps 1–6, but use the Less Than option in step 3.

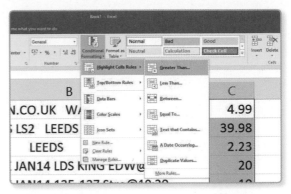

Above: Conditional Formatting is activated in Excel 2007–2016 on the Styles ribbon, which is found on the Home ribbon tab.

Above: Conditional Formatting can help highlight payments into a bank account.

	Amount	Closing balance
ES 6429 LEEDS	-2.64	-36.52
ENCER PLC LEEDS	-8.75	-45.27
X THEAT WELBURN	-32.2	-77.47
USIC LTD LEEDS	-102.96	-180.43
AIRS LTD LEEDS	-31	-211.43
I DD	-182.25	-393.68
ES 5450 HULL	-11.18	-404.86
P 3	-8.45	-413.31
dia	100	-313.31
PET	-48.76	-362.07
	-31.94	-394.01
VW FEB 17	350	-44.01
US A/C JW/FEBRUARY 2017	300	255.99

Above: Conditional Formatting can be used on a bank statement's closing balance column to highlight values less than zero and thus show when the account was overdrawn.

	338.98 zł		$2,20
	342.75 zł	$2,20	
	369.03 zł	$2,20	
	379.18 zł	$2,21	
	394.75 zł	$2,21	
	404.35 zł	$2,21	$1
	414.87 zł	$2,21	$13
	415.60 zł	$2,21	$138
	417.77 zł	$2,21	$140.
	425.02 zł	$2,21	$143,1
	433.00 zł	$2,21	$143,1
	445.70 zł	$2,22	$145.33
	456.72 zł	$2,22	$147.57
	465.42 zł	$2,22	$149.79
	466.87 zł	$2,22	$152.00
	466.87 zł	$2,22	$154.22
	479.57 zł	$2,22	156.445669
	499.15 zł	$2,22	$158.67
	510.02 zł	$2,22	$160.89
	522.52 zł	$2,23	
	543.?? zł	$2.??	

LARGE SPREADSHEETS

MAKING SENSE OF LARGE SPREADSHEETS

It can take some time to understand a large spreadsheet and to locate all the necessary data and calculations. However, there are a few techniques in Excel that can help save a lot of time and frustration.

ADJUSTING THE VIEW

Excel has some quick methods of zooming in and out of spreadsheets, and dividing up the view of one or several spreadsheets – all of which save time on searching and scrolling through data.

Quick Zoom

When working on a spreadsheet, hold down the Ctrl key on the keyboard and rotate the scroll wheel on the mouse. The view of the spreadsheet will quickly zoom in or out, depending on which way the scroll wheel is moved. If the Ctrl key is not held down on the keyboard, the scroll wheel moves up and down the spreadsheet.

Splitting Up

If you need to view data that appears in two different parts of the same worksheet, you can split the sheet into two or four views. For details on how to do this, see the section Moving Around Excel on page 52.

Freezing Panes

Listed or tabled data can often be difficult to understand and read, especially after scrolling down or across the screen, when the headings may have moved out of view. Excel offers a solution to this in Freeze Panes. This allows the headings at the top or left side to stay on the screen when scrolling down or across a worksheet.

Freeze Panes (pre-2007)

To freeze panes in versions of Excel earlier than 2003, select a cell in a spreadsheet where the row above it and the column to the left of it need to remain on screen (frozen). Next, click on the

Hot Tip

Frozen Panes can be spotted in a spreadsheet by a thicker line between the cells.

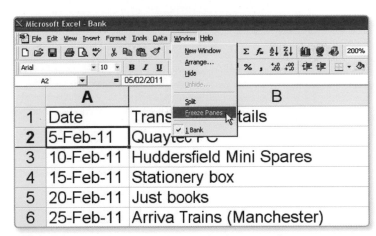

Above: Panes can be frozen in Excel 2003 and earlier versions by clicking on the Window menu.

Window menu and choose Freeze Panes. Scroll down and across the screen to check the correct rows and columns have been frozen. To unfreeze the panes, return to the Window menu and choose the Unfreeze option.

Hot Tip

If you only need to freeze the first two rows but not the columns, select cell A3.

Above: The first row or column in a worksheet can remain visible on screen when frozen, no matter how far down or across the screen you scroll.

Freeze a Column or Row (2007–2016)

If you only want to freeze the top row or first column in a worksheet, select the View ribbon tab and click on the Freeze Panes button in the Window ribbon. A drop-down menu will appear. Select either Freeze Top Row or Freeze First Column. Scroll down or across (depending on

	B	C	Ma			G	H	A
	Jan	Feb				Jun	Jul	
	2450	2450	2450	2450	2450	2450	2450	
		125				150		
	35	35	35	35	35	35	35	

Above: Switch off frozen panes by returning to the menu option or ribbon button used to switch them on.

which option you chose) to make sure the first column or row remains on the screen.

Freeze Multiple Rows and Columns (2007–2016)

Select a cell in the spreadsheet where the row above it and the column to the left of it need to remain on screen. Click on the View ribbon tab, then select Freeze Panes from the Window ribbon. From the drop-down menu that appears, select the first option – Freeze Panes.

Switch Off Frozen Panes (2007–2016)

Frozen panes in Excel 2007–2016 can be switched off by returning to the View ribbon tab, clicking on Freeze Panes and selecting Unfreeze Panes from the drop-down menu.

> ## Hot Tip
> After freezing panes, hold down the Ctrl key on the keyboard and press the Home key to return to the cell directly below the frozen row(s) and/or to the right of the frozen column(s).

VIEWING MORE THAN ONE SPREADSHEET

You can view more than one 'screen' at a time in Excel – whether it's two or more different views of the same worksheet or two or more different workbooks (files) on the screen.

Make a New Window

If only one spreadsheet is open but you need to look at two different areas of it on screen, you can create a

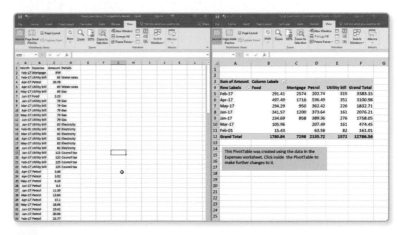

Above: Two or more views of the same worksheet can be set up in Excel by arranging windows.

new window in which to view the second area. In Excel 2003 and earlier versions, click on the Window menu and choose New Window (nothing will happen yet), then return to this menu and select Arrange.

In Excel 2007–2016, click on the View ribbon tab and select the New Window button, then click on the Arrange All button. In all cases, a small box will appear on screen. Choose how you want to organize your views of the spreadsheet, then click on OK.

Working with More Than One Spreadsheet

Two or more spreadsheets can be displayed on screen, which makes it easier to check data and to copy information between files. The steps required to set this up are the same as arranging two views of the same worksheet – you just need to make sure two or more Excel files are open before following the instructions above.

Above: Hidden rows or columns can be revealed by selecting the rows or columns either side, then right-clicking and choosing Unhide.

HIDING ROWS AND COLUMNS

Rows and columns can be hidden to help compress the view of a spreadsheet and see only essential data. Right-click on the column letter or row number and, from the menu that appears, choose Hide. The column or row will disappear from the screen. The hidden column or row can be unhidden by selecting the two columns or rows each side of it, then right clicking inside the selected rows/columns and choosing Unhide.

Hot Tip

Several rows or columns can be hidden at the same time by selecting them, then right clicking on one and choosing Hide.

OUTLINING TOTALS

Excel's Outline tools compress a worksheet down to its subtotals and totals so you can view only essential summary data if you need to. This feature is easy to both add to and remove from a spreadsheet without losing any of the data within it. As long as there is a list of values in a spreadsheet (across or down the screen) with at least one total, the Outline function will work.

Adding Outline (pre-2007)

Make sure the worksheet you are using contains at least one list of numbers with a total calculation (SUM) and then follow these steps:

- Select one cell inside the area of data on the sheet
- Click on the Data menu
- Choose Group and Outline
- Select Auto Outline in the sub-menu
- If any totals have been outlined, number buttons will be displayed in the top left of the grid

Hot Tip

The lowest Outline number button in the top left corner of a spreadsheet displays grand totals. The highest number button displays all the data.

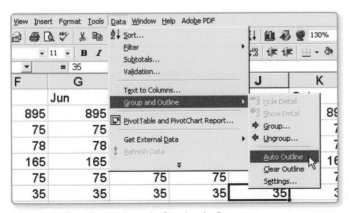

Above: Excel's Outline tools can be found in the Data menu in Excel 2003 and earlier versions.

Above: Click on the Outline number buttons to compress lists of numbers and only display their totals.

→ Click on these number buttons to compress and expand the lists and see the total figures

Adding Outline (2007-2016)

Make sure the worksheet you are using contains at least one list of numbers with a total calculation (SUM) and then follow these steps:

Hot Tip

After switching on Excel's Outline, click on the + and − buttons down the left side of the screen and/or above the column headings.

→ Select one cell inside the area of data
→ Click on the Data ribbon tab near the top of the screen
→ Select the Group button (top right of the screen)
→ Choose Auto Outline from the drop-down menu
→ If any totals have been outlined, number buttons will appear near the top left corner of the grid
→ Click on these buttons to compress and expand the lists and see the total figures

Removing an Outline

To remove an outline in Excel 2007–2016, click on the Ungroup button (next to the Group button) in the Data ribbon tab and select Clear Outline. In earlier versions of Excel, click on the Data menu, choose Group and Outline and select Clear Outline.

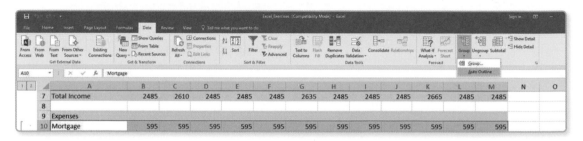

Above: Select the Data ribbon tab, click on the Group button and select Auto Outline to activate the Outline features in Excel 2007–2016.

UNDERSTANDING CALCULATIONS

It can take a while to understand calculations in Excel, especially if someone else has created them. The program offers a number of useful features that can help with this.

Double-Click Check

If you're struggling to figure out how a calculation works, it helps to view the cells to which the calculation relates. To do this, double-click inside the cell containing the calculation and a flashing cursor will appear. Any cells that have been used in the calculation will be highlighted with a coloured border. This is useful for quickly checking totals for lists of numbers. To finish editing the calculation, press Enter/Return on the keyboard (do not select another cell as it may change the calculation).

Expenses				
Mortgage	595	595	595	59
Gas	75	75	75	
Electricity	78	78	78	7
Council tax	150	0	0	10
Water rates	65	65	65	
Telephone	35	35	35	
TV licence	13	13	13	
Sky	45	45	45	
Mobile phone	25	25	25	
Car insurance	120	120	120	12
Petrol	125	125	125	12
Car tax	0	0	0	
Food	500	500	500	50
Clothes	50	50	50	
Eating out + T/ways	75	75	75	
Holidays	0	0	0	
Cash withdrawn	120	80	250	10
Repairs	45	0	0	
Misc	75	56	63	
Total Expenses	=SUM(B10:B28)		2114	218
	SUM(number1, [number2], ...)			
Surplus/Deficit	294	673	371	29

Above: Double-click inside a cell containing a calculation and Excel will highlight the cells used to make up that calculation.

Tracing Calculations

There are two useful toolbar buttons in Excel that can reveal the cells used in a calculation or show whether a cell is used elsewhere in a calculation (particularly handy if you're about to delete the cell). These buttons are called Trace Precedents and Trace Dependents. In Excel 2007–2016, they are displayed on the Formulas ribbon tab within the Formula Auditing section. In earlier versions of Excel, click on the Tools menu, select Auditing or Formula Auditing and then Show Auditing Toolbar.

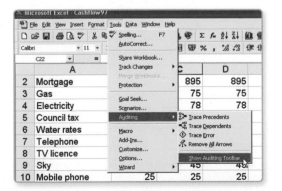

Left: The Formula Auditing Toolbar can be opened via the Tools menu in Excel 2003 and earlier versions.

Is This Cell Used in a Calculation?

It is not always clear whether a cell containing a number has any use, so select it and click on the Trace Dependents button. If the cell's value is used in any calculations, an arrow will lead to those calculations.

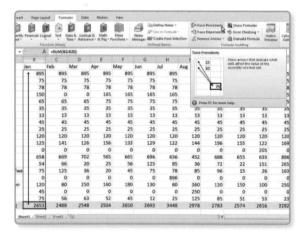

Above: Trace Precedents is useful for finding the cells that affect a calculation.

Finding Cells Used in a Calculation

If a calculation is confusing and difficult to understand, select its cell and click on the Trace Precedents button. All the cells connected with this cell's calculation will be highlighted with a coloured border, and an arrowed line will lead from each cell.

Above: If the screen becomes overloaded with lines and arrows from tracing precedents and dependents, click on the Remove Arrows button.

Removing Lines and Arrows

When using Trace Precedents and Trace Dependents, the screen can quickly become a tangled mess of lines and arrows. To clear the screen, click on the Remove Arrows button. This will not affect the data in the spreadsheet.

LONG LISTS

Excel can store thousands of rows of data, displayed in a long list with headings across the top. It can also help with sorting and filtering this information and creating calculations.

IMPORTING LISTED DATA

Excel can import a variety of data from different programs, ranging from a text file in Word to a report from an Access database. In some cases, an Import Wizard will appear on screen and try to refine the imported data. Sometimes the data will be directly opened in Excel.

Importing Bank Statements

Many banks and building societies offer online banking with the facility to download bank statements. These downloaded statements are sometimes saved as Excel files, but can also be saved as TXT or CSV (comma separated values), which Excel can also open.

Importing TXT or CSV

Excel 2007–2016 provide a number of ribbon buttons on the Get External Data section of the Data ribbon tab. However, the traditional method of opening TXT and CSV files is still available, and this method is applicable to earlier versions of Excel.

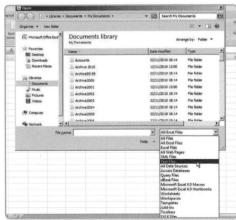

Above: Text files can be opened in Excel via the Open dialogue box.

⊖   **Click on the File menu (the Office button in Excel 2007)**

⊖   **Choose Open to display the Open dialogue box (in Excel 2016, click on Browse)**

- ⮕ **Look for a drop-down list of file types**
- ⮕ **Change this to Text Files**
- ⮕ **Select the file to open**
- ⮕ **Click on the Open button**

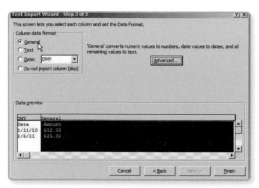

Above: Text files such as downloaded bank statements can be opened in Excel, but sometimes a Text Import Wizard will appear to help determine the structure of the data before opening it.

Copying Non-Excel Data into Excel

Data can usually be selected in another program and copied into Excel. To do this, select the data to be copied and right-click inside the selection. Choose Copy from the menu that appears, then open Excel and right-click inside the cell where the data is to be displayed. Choose Paste from the new menu.

Text Import Wizard

In some cases a Text Import Wizard will appear when you are opening a text file in Excel. This is a series of three dialogue boxes that establish the settings for the text file and decide how the data is separated (spaces, tabs, commas). For further details on this, see the step-by-step guide below on using the Text Import Wizard.

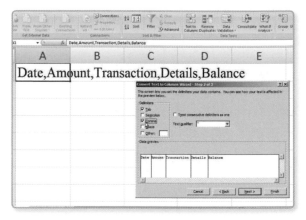

Above: Sometimes, text copied into Excel is squashed into one cell, but needs to be separated out – use the Text to Columns feature for this.

CONVERTING TEXT TO COLUMNS

If data copied into Excel is squashed into one cell when it should be spread across several, select the cell in question and use Text to Columns. This can be found in Excel 2007–2016 by selecting the Data ribbon tab and clicking on the Text to Columns button near the top middle of the screen. In earlier versions of Excel, click on the Data menu and choose Text to Columns. In all cases, a series of three dialogue boxes will appear to establish how the data is separated and what type it is (dates, for example).

STEP-BY-STEP: IMPORTING TEXT FILES

The following step-by-step guide shows how to use the Text Import Wizard to open a text file in Excel and establish how the data is structured. This is useful for downloading bank statements and similar data that has been saved as a text file.

1   Click on the File menu in Excel and choose Open or hold down the Ctrl key on the keyboard and press the letter O. The Open dialogue box will appear on screen (select Browse in Excel 2016). Look for a drop-down box displaying the file type or type of files to open. Click on its drop-down triangle and change the file type to Text Files.

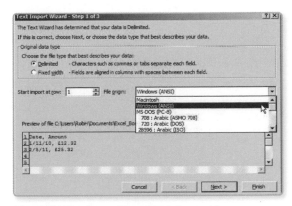

Above: The Text Import Wizard starts by providing options for leaving out data at the top of the text file and how the data should be separated.

Above: The Text Import Wizard can be told whether text file data is separated by commas, tabs or spaces.

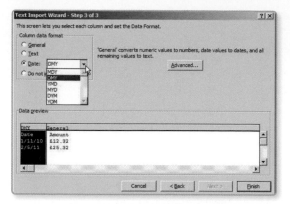

Above: The final stage of the Text Import Wizard provides further choices for data types, so columns can be set to dates, text or general for numbers.

2   Locate the text file to open via the Open dialogue box, select it and click on the Open button. If Excel cannot fully understand the data contained in the text file, the Text Import Wizard will appear. There are three steps to this wizard.

3   The opening dialogue box for the Text Import Wizard helps to determine how the data in the text should be separated (e.g. by commas) or whether each column is a specific size/width. A sample view of the data is shown in the dialogue box, so the settings can be changed and the results seen instantly. This dialogue box also allows you to choose the row number in which the data should be imported, so unwanted headers can be omitted.

4   Click on the Next button to proceed to step 2 of the Text Import Wizard. If the Delimited option was chosen in the last step, you can choose what type of separator is used between each piece of data (comma, semicolon, tab). If Fixed Width was chosen instead, you can click inside the sample view of the text file to set where the data should be separated.

5   The final step of the Text Import Wizard (click on Next if Step 2 of 3 is displayed at the top of the dialogue box) is to choose the data type for each column in the list. Select a column of data from the sample view in the dialogue box, then look at the various format options (General, Text, Date). The layout of the date can also be specified (DMY for date, month, year).

6   If the sample view of the text file's data looks wrong in the Text Import Wizard dialogue box, click on the Back button to return to earlier steps and make any further changes. Otherwise click on Finish. Excel may ask for a location in the spreadsheet to display the text file data or it may open a new workbook, depending on the version of Excel.

MANIPULATING LONG LISTS

Long lists of data often need to be trimmed or refined to extract the important data. This section discusses the tools available in Excel that allow you to filter, sort and summarize information.

FILTERING A LIST

A long table or list of data in Excel can be thinned down using filtering. This does not remove the data, but hides it or extracts specific categories of data based on a search. This is also useful for ranking information to find the best and worst results. Filtering can even be used on a downloaded bank statement to highlight particular transactions (direct debits for a pension, or wages payments, for example) or amounts under/over a specific value.

Instant AutoFilter

Excel's Filter or AutoFilter is one of its most useful features. It displays a series of drop-down menus for each heading in a list, allowing information to be filtered. To switch on the Filter in Excel 2007–2016, make sure one cell is selected inside the list, click on the Data ribbon tab and select the Filter ribbon button near the top middle of the screen. In earlier versions of Excel, select one cell inside the list, then click on the Data menu, choose Filter and select AutoFilter from the sub-menu.

Above: Filter in Excel 2007–2016 is activated via the Data ribbon tab.

Using AutoFilter to Find Information

When AutoFilter is activated, it adds a drop-down menu to each heading in a list. Click on one of these menus and an alphabetical or numerically sorted list of entries from that column will appear. Select one from the list (remove the tick marks in Excel 2007–2016) to display only the rows of data in which this information exists.

Above: AutoFilter provides drop-down menus for each column/heading of a list to help filter specific information.

GREATER AND LESS THAN FILTERING

Lists with dates or numbers often have many rows of data, so AutoFilter can be used to filter specific dates or number ranges. It can also be used to search for values or dates greater than or less than a specific date or amount. This is useful when trying to find unpaid invoices issued before a specific date, for example, or high-value transactions in a bank statement.

Greater and Less Than Filtering (pre-2007)

With AutoFilter switched on, click on the drop-down filter to view a column listing dates or numerical values. Select Custom and a dialogue box will appear. Choose a type of filter method (greater than, less than or equal to), then type a value in the box to the right. Click on OK to close this dialogue box and return to the main screen to see the filtered results. To switch off this filter, return to the drop-down list and choose Select All from the tick-box list.

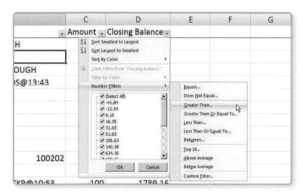

Above: Values greater than and less than a specific amount can be filtered – a useful tool for seeing when a bank account was overdrawn.

Greater and Less Than Filtering (2007–2016)

With AutoFilter switched on, click on the drop-down filter to view a column listing dates or numerical values. Select Number Filters and a sub-menu will appear. Choose one of the search options, such as Greater Than or Between. A dialogue box will appear, allowing specific values to be entered. Click on OK to see the results of the filter. To switch off this filter, return to the drop-down list and choose Select All from the tick-box list.

BEST AND WORST FIGURES

Filtering the best and worst results in a particular column of a list can help to see when a bank account was overdrawn, where sales figures are low and when expenditure is high. This feature is known as the Top 10. To use it, click on the drop-down filter for

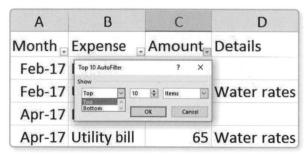

Above: The best and worst values in a list can be filtered using AutoFilter.

a column containing numbers and select Top 10 (in Excel 2007–2016, select Number Filters followed by Top 10 from the sub-menu). From the dialogue box that appears, choose a Top

Hot Tip

Remove a Top 10 filter by clicking on the Clear button on the Data ribbon in Excel 2007–2016 or, in earlier versions of Excel, click on the Data menu, choose Filter and select Show All.

or Bottom filter (best or worst results), followed by the number of results, then click on OK.

WORD FILTERING

Listed data does not always contain the same entries, which can complicate the filtering process. Take a downloaded bank statement as an example. Trying to see all the cash withdrawals is difficult because each transaction description will be different, containing information such as the name of the bank or the time a transaction took place. However, you can use Excel's AutoFilter to find common words displayed in transaction descriptions, such as 'CASH'.

Filter a Word (pre-2007)

Click on the drop-down filter to reveal a column containing text. Choose Custom. From the dialogue box that appears, change the filter type to Contains (near the bottom of the list). Type a word to filter on in the box to the right, then click on OK to see if the filter has worked. To remove this filter, click on the drop-down filter for the relevant column and select (All) at the top of the list.

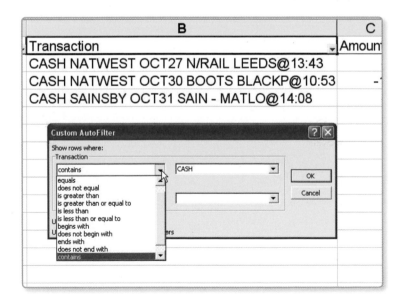

Above: AutoFilter can be used to filter on a specific word in each cell of a particular column.

Filter a Word (2007-2016)

Click on the drop-down filter to reveal a column containing text. Select Text Filters and choose Contains from the sub-menu. A small dialogue box will appear. Type a word to filter inside the box on the right. Click on OK to return to the main screen and check the filter has worked. This filter can be removed by clicking on the Clear button in the middle of the ribbon.

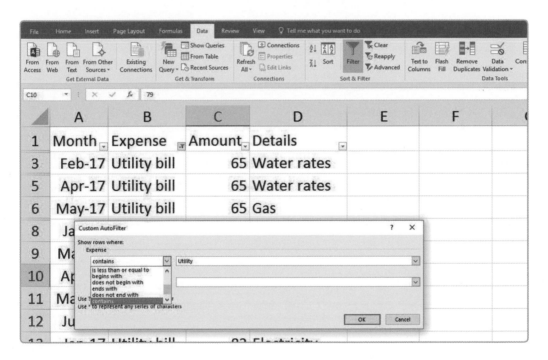

Above: AutoFilter in later versions of Excel works in much the same way.

SWITCH OFF AUTOFILTER

AutoFilter is switched off by repeating the same procedure required to switch it on. In Excel 2007–2016, click on the Filter button in the middle of the Sort & Filter ribbon on the Data tab. In earlier versions of Excel, click on the Data menu, select Filter and choose AutoFilter.

SORTING A LIST

Listed data can be sorted alphabetically or numerically in Excel to help you view information in terms of the highest or lowest figures, for example, or the most recent dates.

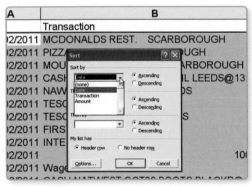

Above: In earlier versions of Excel, the Sort function can be accessed via the Data menu.

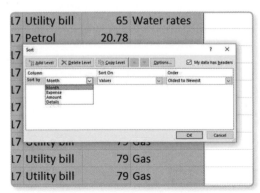

Above: The Sort dialogue box in Excel 2007–2016 displays the headings found in a list and offers a number of ways of sorting the data.

BASIC SORTING

The methods for performing a basic sort function in Excel depend on which version you are using. The following section explains these methods and identifies some of the errors that can occur.

Sorting (pre-2007)

Select one cell inside the table or list of data that needs to be sorted. Click on the Data menu, choose Sort and a Sort dialogue box will open. Click on the drop-down triangle at the top of the dialogue box to reveal a list of column headings. Choose one to sort, then select ascending or descending next to it. Click on OK to return to the spreadsheet and see if the data has been sorted correctly.

Sorting (2007–2016)

Select one cell inside the table or list of data that needs to be sorted. Click on the Data ribbon tab and look for the Sort button in the top middle of the screen (just below the View ribbon tab). Click on this button and a Sort dialogue box will appear

Hot Tip

When using AutoFilter in Excel 2003 and later versions, there are sort options on the drop-down filters for each heading in a list.

containing three criteria boxes with drop-down lists. The first list selects the column heading to sort on, the next one specifies whether the data will be sorted on values or other criteria and the final list decides the sort order. After choosing these options, click on OK to see if the data has been sorted.

Problems with Sorting

Excel will not always identify the cells contained inside a list, so column headings may be missed out or data will not be sorted. If this happens, try selecting the data before opening the Sort dialogue box. Quick methods for selecting cells were covered in the previous chapter. If Excel does not recognize the column headings and consequently sorts them, double check to ensure there is a tick against Header Row in the Sort dialogue box.

FAST SORTING

Excel has two Sort toolbar buttons on the Data ribbon tab in Excel 2007–2016 and on the Standard toolbar in earlier versions. They have the letters AZ or ZA displayed on them with an arrow pointing up or down (meaning 'sort ascending' or 'sort descending'). For fast sorting, select a cell inside the column to be sorted, then click on one of these buttons. If only a single column is sorted and not the rest of the list, click on the Undo button and use the Sort dialogue box instead.

Hot Tip

Undo is a lifesaver when something goes wrong because it reverses the mistake made. Undo can be quickly activated by holding down the Ctrl key on the keyboard and pressing the letter Z.

MULTIPLE SORTING

Excel can sort on more than one heading. For example, a list of sales results could be sorted in date order, but within each date the sales values can be ordered numerically. In Excel 2007–2016, click on the Add Level button in the Sort dialogue box and an extra row of sort criteria will be displayed. In earlier versions of Excel, the Sort dialogue box automatically offers up to three sorting levels.

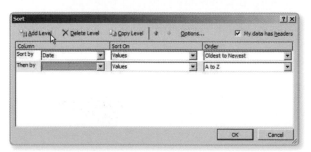

Above: Click on the Add Level button in the Sort dialogue box for Excel 2007–2016 to sort on more than one column heading.

SORT BY COLOUR (2007–2016)

Lists of data can often be easier to understand if cells are colour coded. For example, unpaid invoices could be coloured in either red, orange or green to signify those that need attention. If cells are coloured (fill colour), Excel 2007–2016 can sort them according to their colours. When using the Sort dialogue box, change the Sort On (middle list) to Cell Colour, then specify which colour to sort on in the next drop-down list. Click on the Add Level button to enter further sort criteria for other colours. For further information on this, see the step-by-step guide below.

STEP-BY-STEP: SORTING COLOURED CELLS IN EXCEL 2007–2016

The following step-by-step guide shows how to create a to-do list, add fill colours to the cells and sort them according to the colouring. This method of sorting is only available in Excel 2007–2016.

1 Open Excel and start up a new blank workbook. Enter a heading in cell A1, such as 'Jobs to do'. Enter the heading 'Location' in cell B1 (here you will input house, garden, car, garage, for example) and finally enter a third heading in cell C1 for 'Date entered', so you can see how long that job has been pending. If necessary, a fourth column could be useful for comments, so add a suitable heading in cell D1.

2 Widen columns A and B by positioning the mouse pointer between these column letters. When the pointer changes to a black cross with horizontal arrows, hold down the left button and drag to the right to widen column A. Release the left button to stop widening it. Repeat the same process for column B by positioning the mouse pointer between column letters B and C (the same can be done for column C).

3 Enter a few sample jobs, along with a location and the date each job was listed. Excel's AutoComplete will help when typing a location that has already been entered. For instance, if the word House has already been entered, you only have to type the letter 'H' and the word 'House' will appear (press Enter/ Return to confirm).

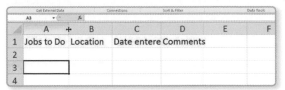

Above: Widen the columns by positioning the mouse pointer between the column letters and dragging it to the right.

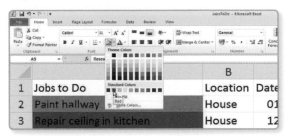

Above: Excel will try to AutoComplete entries in a list based on entries above the selected cell.

Above: Excel's Fill Colour offers a palette of colours, which are useful for colour-coding a list prior to sorting it.

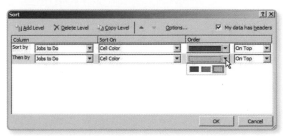

Above: The Sort dialogue box allows multiple sort criteria to be added, so the colour-coded cells can be sorted in a particular order.

4   Save the Excel file with a meaningful name (e.g. JobsToDo). Click on the Home ribbon tab and look for the Font ribbon near the top left of the screen. Inside this section is a small Fill Colour toolbar button, which looks like a bucket with a colour underneath it. Click on the tiny drop-down triangle next to it and a palette of colours will appear.

5   A colour-coding scheme of red (needs immediate attention), orange (quite important) and green (can wait) can be applied to the job descriptions in column A. Select one cell at a time, click on the Fill Colour drop-down triangle and choose the appropriate colour.

6   After applying the various fill colours to the cells in column A, this list can be sorted according to the colours. Make sure one cell is selected in the list, then click on the Data ribbon tab and select the Sort button near the top middle of the screen. The Sort dialogue box will appear on the screen.

7   Using the Sort dialogue box, click on the drop-down list for Sort by Section (far left) and choose column A's heading (e.g. Jobs to do). Click on the next drop-down list for Sort On and select Cell Colour. Next, choose a colour that has been used from the list on the left. This colour will be top of the sorted list, as long as the option next to it states 'On Top'.

8   After setting up one colour to be sorted, the order of the other colours can be established. Click on the Add Level button in the Sort dialogue box. A second sort criterion will appear. Change the settings using the drop-down lists to sort another colour. Continue adding more levels until all the colours are sorted, then click on OK to check that the list is sorted correctly.

Hot Tip

Click on the Delete Level button in the Sort dialogue box to remove any sort criteria.

Hot Tip

Switch on Excel's Filter and 'Sort by Colour' is listed on any drop-down filters where the cells are colour coded.

TALLYING DATA

Listed data can be grouped together and summarized to show you totals and other calculations. A list of expenses, for example, can be summarized according to types of expenses and totals per month. Excel has a number of features for summarizing listed data, including Subtotals and Pivot Tables.

SUBTOTALS

Once you have a list in Excel you can manipulate it in various ways to reveal different information. One of the most useful functions when working with basic lists is Subtotals. The sections below explain how to use Excel to reveal subtotals from lists or tables in different formats.

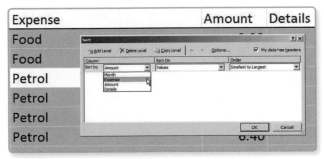

Above: A list needs to be sorted before it can be subtotalled to ensure that data is correctly grouped.

Sort It First

Excel's Subtotals requires a list of data to be sorted so that particular types of information in one column are grouped correctly. This makes it easier to apply subtotals to the list. In a list of expenses, the expense type column could be sorted so that all different categories of expenses (mortgage, utility bills, food, petrol) are grouped and can thus be subtotalled. For information on how to sort data lists in this way, see page 114.

Choose the Numbers

Once a list of data has been sorted so that all the items in a particular column are grouped, make sure you have at least one column containing numbers that can be subtotalled. In a list of expenses, this might be the amount of each expense. In a list of sales, where there are columns for net amounts, VAT and gross amounts, it could be one, two or all three of these columns.

Above: In Excel 2007–2016, Subtotals is activated via the Data ribbon tab and the Subtotals ribbon button.

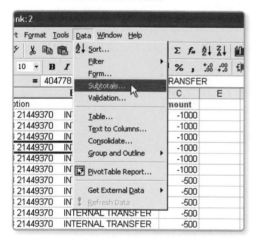

Above: In Excel 2003 and earlier versions, Subtotals is activated via the Data menu.

Subtotals Dialogue Box

The Subtotals dialogue box is the same in all versions of Excel. It contains three main sections. Starting at the top, choose the column heading that has been sorted and grouped. In the section

Switch on Subtotals

Select one cell inside the listed data or, to be safe, select all the data to be included in the subtotal, including the column headings. In Excel 2007–2016, click on the Data ribbon tab and select the Subtotal ribbon button near the top right of the screen. In earlier versions of Excel, click on the Data menu and choose Subtotals. In both cases, a Subtotals dialogue box will appear.

Hot Tip

Select all the data inside a list by clicking in one cell inside the list, then holding down the Ctrl and Shift keys together and pressing the space bar.

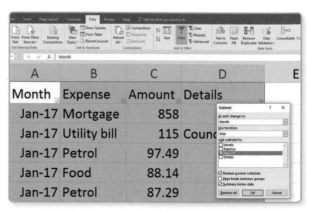

Above: Excel's Subtotals can calculate groups of data as long as the information is sorted correctly.

under 'Use function', choose a calculation to apply (e.g. Sum or Average). In the next section ('Add subtotal to'), make sure there is at least one tick mark against a column heading that contains numbers. Remove any tick marks against columns that don't have numbers (Excel sometimes adds them by accident). Click on OK to see if the Subtotals have been correctly applied.

Hot Tip

You can add more than one tick mark to the 'Add subtotal to' list when applying Subtotals.

Using Subtotals

Once Subtotals have been applied to a list of data, you should see a series of numbered buttons near the top left corner of the spreadsheet. Click on these buttons to expand and collapse the listed data. The highest numbered button will display all the data and the lowest number will display a grand total. You can also click on the plus and minus symbols down the left side of the screen to expand and collapse sections of data.

Above: After applying Subtotals to a list, click on the + and – symbols down the left side of the screen to expand and contract groups of data.

Non-Numerical Subtotals

Subtotals can be applied to lists that don't contain any numbers. The data can be grouped and counted. After sorting the information into relevant groups, open the Subtotals dialogue box and, under the Use function, choose Count. This is useful when managing a to-do list, where subtotals can show how many jobs there are for the house, garden, garage and car.

Subtotals within Subtotals

A list can have more than one level of subtotals. For example, a list of household expenses can have subtotals for the expenditure per month, but within this grouping there could be

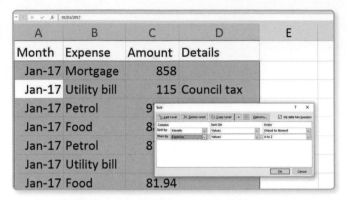

Above: You can create Subtotals within Subtotals, but the data has to be correctly sorted first.

Hot Tip

The data in a list is not affected by applying or removing Subtotals.

subtotals for how much has been spent on food, petrol and utility bills. Setting this up requires the listed data to be sorted on two levels (by month and then by the type of expense). For detailed information on this, see the Step-by-Step guide on page 128.

Removing Subtotals

Subtotals can be quickly removed, no matter how many have been set up. Make sure one cell is selected inside the list of data, then reopen the Subtotals dialogue box and click on the button labelled Remove All.

PIVOTTABLES

While Excel's Subtotals are useful for grouping and tallying data within a list, PivotTables are more powerful and can summarize data in a separate area of a spreadsheet without risking anything happening to the original data.

Understanding PivotTables

PivotTables are one of the best features of Excel, but can appear bewildering to

Sum of Amount	Column				
Row Labels	Food	Mortgage	Petrol	Utility	Grand Total
Feb-17	291.41		2574	202.7	315	3383.15
Apr-17	497.49		1716	536.5	351	3100.98
May-17	294.29		950	362.4	226	1832.71
Jun-17	341.57		1200	373.6	161	2076.21
Jan-17	234.69		858	389.4	276	1758.05
Mar-17	105.96			207.5	161	474.45
Feb-01	15.43			63.58	82	161.01
Grand Total	1780.8		7298	2136	1572	12786.56

Above: Subtotals can be added below and to the right of a table of data.

the beginner. They should only be used for listed data – but that list can be as simple as a downloaded bank statement or a list of expenses, or as complex as downloaded sales data containing product codes and retail outlets.

What Is a PivotTable?

A PivotTable uses a list of data to group and tally its information and create a table of results. It can summarize thousands of lines of information in a list into one simple table that adds up similar categories of information. Years of utility bills, mortgage payments and pension contributions can be totalled in a PivotTable.

Check and Select PivotTable Data

It is important to ensure you're using the correct type of data when creating a PivotTable, otherwise it will not work correctly. Listed data is ideal, with headings across the top of the spreadsheet and the information listed down the screen, with few or no blank cells and no blank rows. It is good practice to select all the data before creating a PivotTable.

Creating a PivotTable (2007-2016)

Follow these steps to create a PivotTable in the most recent versions of Excel.

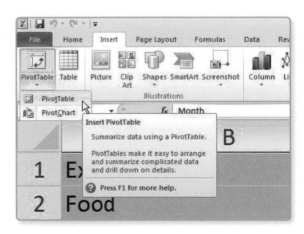

- ➔ **Click on the Insert ribbon tab**
- ➔ **Select the PivotTable ribbon button near the top left corner of the screen**
- ➔ **A Create PivotTable dialogue box will appear – check the range of cells displayed is correct**
- ➔ **Decide on the location for the PivotTable (a new worksheet will appear in the workbook being used)**

Above: Start creating a PivotTable in Excel 2007–2016 by clicking on the Insert ribbon tab and selecting the drop-down triangle in the top left corner of the screen. (For Excel 2016, just click on the PivotTable button.)

Click on OK

 A blank PivotTable will appear on the left side of the screen, with a number of options displayed on the right

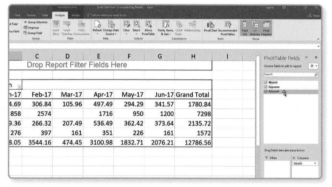

Above: Select the column headings (fields) on the right side of the screen in Excel 2007–2016 to add them to a PivotTable.

Above: The type of calculation used in a PivotTable can be changed to display the average values, highest (Max) or lowest (Min).

Building a PivotTable (2007–2016)

After creating an empty PivotTable, add tick marks to the list of column headings on the right side of the screen (under PivotTable Fields). Data will then be added to the PivotTable, but it may be in the wrong location. Look at the bottom right corner of the screen. The column headings will be displayed under Row Labels, Column Labels or Values. Drag and drop the column headings between these sections to change the layout of the PivotTable.

Changing the PivotTable Calculation (2007–2016)

The type of calculation used in a PivotTable is usually a Sum function for numbers or a Count for non-numerical data. This can be changed by right-clicking in a cell showing a calculation (a value) inside the PivotTable. Choose

Value Field Settings from the menu that appears and a dialogue box will be displayed. Choose a different type of calculation from the list inside this dialogue box and click on OK.

Hot Tip

Not sure whether a value inside a PivotTable is correct? Double-click on it and all the data that has been used to calculate that value will be displayed in a new worksheet.

Creating a PivotTable (pre-2007)

Click on the Data menu and select PivotTable Report (some Excel versions have a longer name). A PivotTable Wizard dialogue box will appear on screen, consisting of four steps. The first step decides the location of the data to be included in the PivotTable. If the data is in the Excel worksheet on screen, make sure the option labelled Microsoft Excel list or database is selected, then click on Next. The cell range for the data also needs to be specified – Excel often does this automatically, but check that the cell range is correct before clicking on Next.

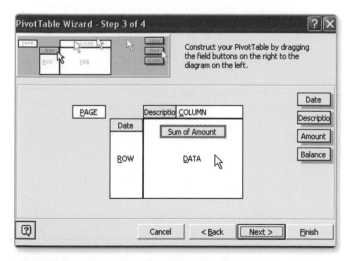

Above: Earlier versions of Excel (pre-2007) use a PivotTable Wizard that helps construct a PivotTable before it appears on screen.

Excel pre-2007 PivotTable Differences

The third dialogue box in the PivotTable Wizard differs depending on which version of Excel you are using. Early versions of Excel display a layout of the PivotTable, whereas later versions require you to click on the Layout button. In all cases, the structure of the PivotTable can be created by dragging and dropping the field/column headings into the areas of the PivotTable. Drag and drop a column heading containing numbers into the Data section. The Row and Column sections of the PivotTable should use column headings where the data can be grouped (e.g. month or expense type).

Hot Tip

If the toolbar and other PivotTable options have disappeared, you only need to select one cell inside the PivotTable to display them on screen.

Adding a PivotTable to a New or Existing Worksheet

A PivotTable can be displayed in a new or existing worksheet. While Excel 2007–2016 provides this option at the beginning of the set-up process, earlier versions of Excel display this option at the end of the PivotTable Wizard. After making the choice, click on Finish and the PivotTable will appear on screen.

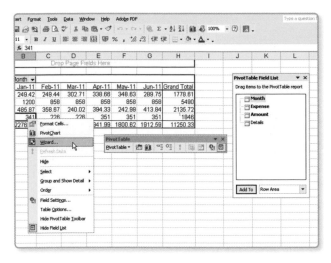

Above: PivotTables can be modified by right-clicking inside them and using an assortment of options on the shortcut menu.

WORKING WITH PIVOTTABLES

Once you have set up an empty PivotTable and established the criteria for the data it includes, you will need to know how to modify the data, amend calculations and refresh the information.

Modifying a PivotTable (pre-2007)

A PivotTable toolbar will appear when a PivotTable is created and at least one cell inside it is selected. There are also numerous options available by right-

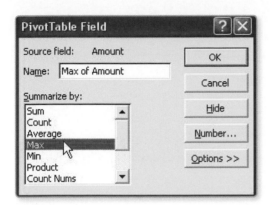

Above: To change the type of calculation, choose Value Field or Field Settings – a dialogue box similar to the one shown here will appear.

clicking on a cell inside the PivotTable. For example, you can return to the PivotTable Wizard by right-clicking inside the table and choosing Wizard.

Changing the PivotTable Calculation (pre-2007)

The type of calculation used in a PivotTable is usually a Sum function for numbers or a Count for non-numerical data. This can be changed by right-clicking in a cell showing a calculation (a value) inside the PivotTable. Choose Value Field or Field Settings –

depending on the version of Excel you are using – from the menu that appears and a dialogue box will be displayed. Choose a different type of calculation from the list and click on OK.

Refreshing PivotTable Data

PivotTables are not automatically updated, so if a cell in a list is changed the PivotTable will need to be updated. This can be executed quickly using the Refresh function. The fastest method of refreshing a PivotTable is to right-click inside it and choose Refresh from the menu that appears. However, in Excel 2007–2016, there is a Refresh

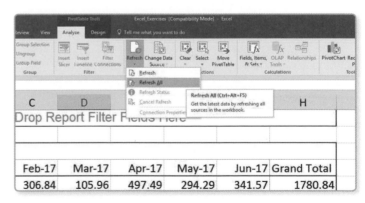

Above: PivotTables don't automatically update themselves, so click on the Refresh button.

button on the Options ribbon tab, and in earlier versions of Excel there is a Refresh toolbar button, which looks like a red exclamation mark.

STEP-BY-STEP: SUBTOTALLING EXPENSES LISTS

A list of expenses, money paid in, or any list in which there are dates, values and categories relating to each value, can all be summarized in Excel using Subtotals. The following step-by-step guide shows how to apply two levels of Subtotals.

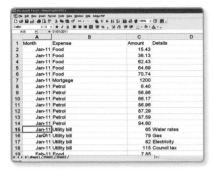

Above: Enter the data as a list, with headings across the top; this format makes it easier for Excel to apply Subtotals.

Above: In Excel 2003 and earlier versions, there are up to three levels of sorting available, enabling levels of Subtotals to be applied.

1 If you don't have a list to use, enter four headings in cells A1, B1, C1 and D1 for the words Month, Expense, Amount and Details. Type some sample data down the screen (see the illustrations for suggestions) and make sure the dates in column A are the same for each month, such as Jan 11 or Mar 11.

2 The list of data needs to be sorted according to Month and then according to Expense. This will allow two levels of Subtotals to be entered. Select one cell inside the list, then click on the Data menu or ribbon and choose Sort. A dialogue box will appear.

3 Set the criteria in the Sort dialogue box to sort by Month (Ascending or Oldest to Newest), then by Expense (Ascending or A to Z) – in Excel 2007–2016 click on the Add Level button to add another sort criteria. Click on OK to close the dialogue box and check whether the list has been correctly sorted.

4 The months in column A should be listed in date order, but the expense types in column B should only be sorted within each month (scroll down to check). We can now apply the Subtotals, so select one cell in the list, then click on the Data menu or ribbon and select Subtotal from the menu or toolbar button (Excel 2007–2016). A Subtotal dialogue box will appear.

5 Make sure Month is displayed in the first option in the Sort dialogue box. Under Use function, choose Sum (this will add up values). Add a tick mark to Amount in the list below, but remove any other tick marks. Click on OK to close the dialogue box. Subtotals will now have been applied to each month with totals displayed in the Amount column.

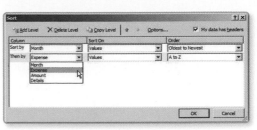

Above: In the Sort dialogue box for Excel 2007–2016, click on the Add Level button to sort on more than one level.

6 A second Subtotal can now be added, so make sure one cell is selected inside the list, then reopen the Subtotals dialogue box. Remove the tick mark from the option labelled Replace Current Subtotals. Now change the criteria to read Expense for the first option, Sum for the function and keep a tick mark against Amount. Click on OK to close the dialogue box.

7 After closing the Subtotals dialogue box, there should be four buttons in the top left corner of the spreadsheet. Click on the second button to see totals for each month and a grand total. The third button displays the totals for each expense per month, plus a monthly total. The first button displays only a grand total and the fourth displays all the data.

Above: The Subtotal dialogue box enables calculations to be made on specific columns, which can be based on groups of data in another column.

8 Click on the plus and minus (+ and –) symbols down the left side of the screen to expand and collapse the list and the see the subtotals. To switch off the Subtotals, return to the dialogue box and click on Remove All.

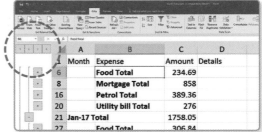

Above: After applying Subtotals, click on the numbered buttons in the top left corner of the screen to change the view of the list and expand/collapse data.

STEP-BY-STEP: MAKING A PIVOTTABLE FROM EXPENSES (2007–2016)

It takes practice to understand PivotTables, so the following step-by-step guide takes a simple list of expenses and demonstrates how to transform it into a summary in the form of a PivotTable. With a little practice, complex lists with thousands of rows of data can be quickly summarized into one small PivotTable.

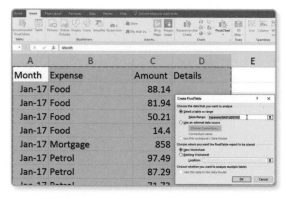

Above: Check that the Table/Range cell references cover the list in the Create PivotTable dialogue box; if they are wrong, click inside the white box and select the correct cells.

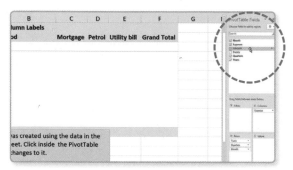

Above: Add ticks against Month, Expense and Amount – after adding the column headings, the structure may not be suitable, but this can be modified.

1 If you don't have a list to use, enter four headings in cells A1, B1, C1 and D1 with the words Month, Expense, Amount and Details. Type some sample data down the screen (see the illustrations for suggestions) and make sure the dates in column A use the same format for each month, such as Jan 11 or Mar 11.

2 Select the entire list by choosing one cell, then holding down the Ctrl and Shift keys on the keyboard and pressing the space bar. Next, click on the Insert ribbon tab, then select the PivotTable ribbon button in the top left corner of the screen.

Hot Tip
PivotTable data is not automatically updated, so right click inside the PivotTable and choose Refresh.

3 A Create PivotTable dialogue box will appear. Make sure the cell references for Table/Range are correct (don't worry about the $ signs) and that New Worksheet is selected, then click on OK.

4 A new blank PivotTable will appear inside a new worksheet of the existing workbook/file (look at the sheet tabs to check). Add tick marks against Month, Expense and Amount, which are listed near the top right corner of the screen.

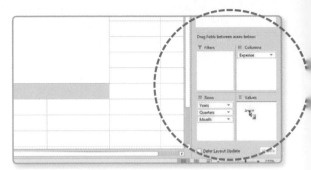

Above: Drag and drop the column/field headings between the boxes in the bottom right corner of the screen to change the layout of the PivotTable.

5 The PivotTable will be instantly constructed after clicking on each field in the last step. However, the structure can probably be improved, so look at the bottom right corner of the screen. Drag and drop the Month heading under Row Labels over to the Column Labels box.

m of Amount	Column Labels		Mortgage	Petrol
w Labels	Foo			
2017				
Jan			858	389.3
Feb			2574	266.3
Mar				207.4
Apr			1716	536.4
May			950	362.4
Jun		341.57	1200	373.6

Above: Click on the AutoFilter drop-down triangles to open a filter list and select or eliminate data from the PivotTable.

6 With the PivotTable correctly constructed, try clicking on the AutoFilter triangles next to Row Labels and Column Labels (inside the PivotTable). A menu will drop down, allowing specific months or expense categories to be filtered.

7 PivotTables can be removed from a spreadsheet by either selecting the respective cells and pressing Delete on the keyboard, or by right-clicking on the PivotTable's sheet tab and choosing Delete (all the data in that sheet will be lost).

STEP-BY-STEP: MAKING A PIVOTTABLE FROM EXPENSES (PRE-2007)

The following step-by-step guide takes a simple list of expenses and shows you how to transform it into a summary in the form of a PivotTable. The instructions and illustrations apply to the versions of Excel from 5.0 to 2003, although screen pictures and some menu options may differ slightly in places.

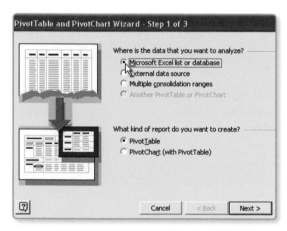

Above: Creating a PivotTable in Excel 2003 and earlier versions involves the use of a series of dialogue boxes; start by specifying the location of the data to be used in the PivotTable.

Above: It's essential to ensure Excel has the correct cell references for the list used to make a PivotTable.

1 If you don't have a list to use, enter four headings in cells A1, B1, C1 and D1 for the words Month, Expense, Amount and Details. Type some sample data down the screen (see the illustrations for suggestions) and make sure the dates in column A use the same format for each month, such as Jan 11 or Mar 11.

2 Select the entire list by choosing one cell, then holding down the Ctrl and Shift keys on the keyboard and pressing the space bar. Next, click on the Data menu and choose PivotTable Report (the words vary according to the Excel version you are using). A PivotTable Wizard dialogue box will appear.

3 Make sure the option for using a Microsoft Excel list or database is selected, then click on Next. In the second dialogue box, check the cell references for the list are correct (don't worry about the $ signs), then

click on Next. In the third box, click on the Layout button (Excel 2000–2003).

4 The structure of the PivotTable can now be decided. Drag and drop the Month from the right side over to the COLUMN section. Take the Expense box to the ROW section and the Amount box into the DATA area (this will be changed to Sum of Amount). Click on OK to return to the previous dialogue box.

5 Make sure New Worksheet is selected, then click on Finish to close the dialogue box and see the PivotTable displayed on a new worksheet within the existing workbook/file.

6 The PivotTable can be further modified using the PivotTable toolbar or by right-clicking inside the PivotTable. Data can be filtered by clicking on the drop-down triangles next to Month and Expense to choose or omit particular information.

7 PivotTables can be removed from a spreadsheet by either selecting the respective cells and pressing Delete on the keyboard, or by right-clicking on the PivotTable's sheet tab and choosing Delete (all the data in that sheet will be lost).

Above: Click on the Layout button to create the structure of the PivotTable.

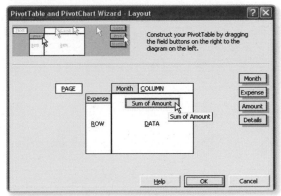

Above: Drag and drop column/field headings into the PivotTable to construct it.

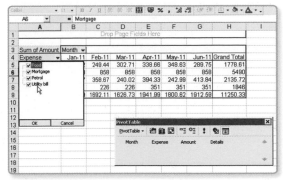

Above: PivotTables can be manipulated without damaging the original data list; click on the drop-down triangles to filter categories of data.

CREATING CALCULATIONS

MAKING YOUR OWN CALCULATIONS

Calculations can be written into a cell in Excel, but there are some important rules to be aware of and some potential problems that can arise. This section takes you through the basics you'll need to know in order to use Excel's calculation features, as well as highlighting the pitfalls to watch out for.

BASIC RULES

There are a couple of fundamental rules you should get to grips with before starting on Excel calculations. After a bit of practice, however, they should become second nature.

Use the = Sign

One of the most important things to remember when inputting calculations into Excel is they must always begin with an equals (=) sign. This tells Excel that a calculation is being added, rather than text. For example, if you enter A1+B1 into a cell without the = sign at the beginning, then the text A1+B1 will be displayed rather than the intended calculation.

	A	B	C	E	F
1	Net	P&P	VAT		
2	100	10	=A2+B2*17.5%		
3	100	10	19.25		
4					
5					
6					

Above: When writing a calculation, any cells included will be highlighted with a coloured border.

Select the Cells

When inputting a calculation, use the mouse to select the cells you want to include. This will make sure that the correct cells are chosen and eliminate the risk of errors. In most versions of Excel, the cell and its reference in the calculation will be colour-coded when you are inputting the information.

MATHEMATICAL SYMBOLS

Excel uses the standard set of computer-based mathematical symbols for calculations, which are not the same as the non-computer mathematical symbols. While the + and - symbols are used for addition and subtraction, the multiplication symbol is an asterisk (*), not an x. The division symbol is the forward slash (/). All these mathematical symbols can be found on the number pad on a standard keyboard. If you are using a laptop, the symbols can be found as follows:

Hot Tip

On some laptops, the symbols normally found on the number pad are displayed in a different colour on other keys. The symbol can usually be activated by holding down a Fn or Mode key.

- **+ To the left of the Backspace key and includes the = symbol (hold down the Shift key to use it, otherwise an = symbol will appear)**
- **- To the left of the = and + key**
- **/ Near the bottom right of the keyboard and includes the ? symbol**
- *** Hold down the Shift key and press the number 8 (along the top of the keyboard)**

BODMAS RULES

BODMAS is a mathematical rule concerning the order of a calculation in relation to the mathematical symbols used. The abbreviation stands for:

- **B**rackets
- **O**f
- **D**ivision
- **M**ultiplication
- **A**ddition
- **S**ubtraction

Above: The calculation in C2 is wrong because the rule of BODMAS means 10 is multiplied by 17.5% first, whereas the calculation needs to add 100 and 10 first – adding brackets resolves this, as shown in C3.

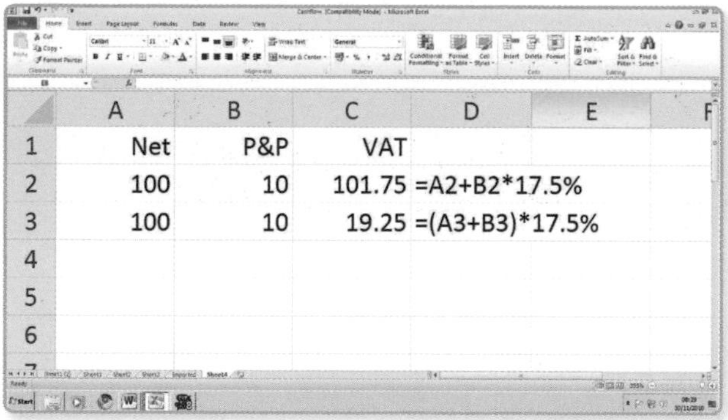

BODMAS is a priority rule for calculations. Anything in brackets is calculated first, and within those brackets anything with a

Hot Tip

When copying a calculation down a table or list using AutoFill, double click the left button on the mouse when the pointer is a small black cross. AutoFill will instantly copy the calculation into the cells below.

division or multiplication symbol is calculated before anything with an addition or subtraction. If there are no brackets, then divisions and multiplications are calculated before additions and subtractions.

How BODMAS Works

The easiest way to understand this rule is to look at an example. Take a typical order when buying something on the internet. The net price is usually listed, followed by a charge for postage and packing, then a calculation for VAT. Imagine the net price is £100 and the postage is £10. If a calculation to work out the amount of VAT is written as =100+10*17.5%, then the rule of BODMAS means multiplication comes first, so 10 will be multiplied by 17.5%. However, we need to add 100 and 10 together before multiplying by 17.5%, so the calculation needs to be written as =(100+10)*17.5%.

CALCULATE AND COPY

Calculations created in a table or list can be copied using Excel's AutoFill. If

Above: Calculations can be copied down or across a table or list using AutoFill, as long as the structure of the calculation remains the same.

the structure of the calculation is the same across or down a table or list, then copying one calculation using AutoFill will change the cell references for each copied calculation. This can save hours of typing and reduces the risk of mistakes when re-writing a calculation.

DOLLAR SIGNS

Some calculations are created with dollar signs next to the cell references. These are known as 'absolute cell references' and mean that part or all of the cell reference will not change if it is copied or Autofilled elsewhere. It can be useful when a number of calculations are created using one particular cell, such as a single VAT value. If VAT

	A	B	C	D	E
1	Product	Price	VAT	17.50%	
2	Keyboard	£7.99	=B2*D1		
3	Mouse	£4.99			
4	Mouse mat	£2.50			
5	Monitor	£79.99			
6	Scanner	£74.99			
7					

Above: Adding dollar signs to the cell reference for D1 means that when the calculation is copied down the table, the reference to D1 won't change, while the reference to B2 will change (to B3, B4 etc).

changes, then there will only be one cell to change. This is helpful in sales spreadsheets, but is also handy for forecasting where mark-up values can be used and changed.

When to Use Dollar Signs

If a list of product prices needs an adjacent column with a calculation for VAT, then a single cell can display the VAT amount. In the example pictured, cell D1 contains the VAT value. When the first VAT calculation is written in cell C2, it should read =B2*D1, but if this calculation is copied down the table, then the VAT calculation for the Mouse in C3 would read =B3*D2, which is wrong (D2 is empty). By changing the first calculation to read =B2*D1, when copied down the table the cell reference for D1 won't change, but the cell reference for B2 will change to B3, B4, and so on.

Hot Tip

Dollar signs can be quickly added when writing a calculation. After selecting the cell in which to include dollar signs, press **F4** on the keyboard. Note that this only works when writing a calculation.

ADDING, AVERAGING AND COUNTING

Straightforward calculations – including adding up lists of numbers, finding an average or revealing the highest and lowest values – can be quickly created or displayed in Excel. This section explains everything you need to know about basic calculations.

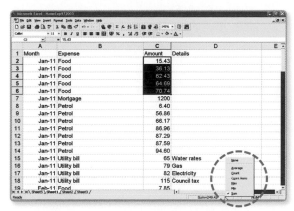

Above: Select a range of cells in Excel 97 or later versions and a calculation of those cells will be displayed on the status bar.

QUICK CALCULATIONS ON THE STATUS BAR

The status bar is displayed at the bottom of the screen and can be used to show a number of calculations based on a selection of cells (in versions of Excel later than 1997). First, select a range of cells containing numbers. Next, look along the bottom right edge of the screen. A calculation such as SUM will be displayed with a value next to it based on the selected cells (several calculations are displayed in Excel 2007/2010). Right-click here to change the type of calculation shown.

Hot Tip

If the status bar isn't displayed at the bottom of the screen in Excel 2003 or earlier versions, click on the View menu and make sure there is a tick mark against Status bar.

AUTOSUM

Excel's AutoSum toolbar button, which has a Greek Sigma symbol displayed on it (Σ), was originally used to add up lists of numbers based on a selection of cells, or on Excel assuming the cells to add up were above or to the left of the selected cell. In Excel 2002 this was changed so that the AutoSum toolbar button had a drop-down menu with additional calculations, including Average, Max (highest values) and Min (lowest values).

Above: Excel 2016 includes Quick Analysis tools to help calculate a total. Select some cells and this will appear below as a Smart Tag.

Using AutoSum to Add Lists of Numbers

Select an empty cell at the bottom of a list of numbers or to the right of a row of numbers. Click on the AutoSum toolbar button (in Excel 2007–2016 this is on the Home ribbon tab) and Excel will automatically create an =SUM calculation with the cell range above or to the right of the selected cell. Press Enter/Return on the keyboard to complete the calculation. In Excel 2016, Quick Analysis Tools can also be used to create totals (see above illustration).

AutoSum an Entire Table

If you want to add totals at the bottom and/or right of a table of

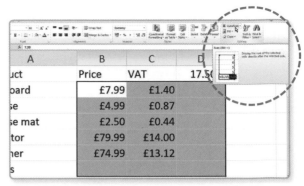

Hot Tip

If the cell references are incorrect, all you need to do is select the correct ones to overwrite the calculation.

Above: Select the values inside a table of data, as well as the empty cells below and to the right of these, then click on the AutoSum button to instantly add SUM totals.

numbers, you can do so in AutoSum with one click. First, select the table of numbers and an empty row of cells below it and/or an empty column of cells to the right of it. Click once on the AutoSum button and the SUM totals will be added to the empty cells selected.

Other Calculations with AutoSum (2002–2016)

The AutoSum toolbar or ribbon button has a drop-down menu in Excel 2002 and later versions. This menu lists other calculations (functions), most of which can be created in the same way as an addition calculation. Some of the useful calculations on the AutoSum drop-down menu include:

- **Average**: This calculates the mean average value based on a selection of cells.
- **Count or Count Numbers**: This counts the number of cells containing numbers.
- **Max**: This displays the highest number in a range of cells.
- **Min**: This displays the lowest number in a range of cells.

Using Other Calculations

An average can be calculated by selecting a list of cells containing numbers and an empty cell at the bottom. Click on the drop-down triangle on the AutoSum button and choose Average from the menu that appears. The calculation will be created in the empty cell at the bottom of the list.

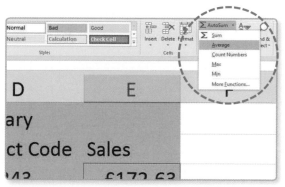

Displaying a Calculation Elsewhere

If a calculation such as Sum, Average or Count does not need to be displayed at the bottom or

Above: The AutoSum toolbar or ribbon button has a drop-down menu of other calculations in Excel 2002 and later versions.

side of a list of numbers, you can still use the AutoSum button or its drop-down menu. Select the cell in which the calculation should be displayed, then click on the AutoSum button or its drop-down triangle and choose a calculation. The calculation will be displayed with an incorrect cell range. Choose the correct cells using the mouse and the range will be displayed in the calculation. Press Enter/Return on the keyboard to finish the calculation.

BASIC FUNCTIONS

Excel has a number of in-built, ready-to-use calculations called functions. These save time in typing out calculations by hand and have a wide range of uses, including statistical analysis, finding data in a list and error checking.

ADDING A FUNCTION TO A CELL

A function is entered and displayed inside a cell just like any other calculation. One of the quickest methods of adding a function to a cell was covered in the last section – using the AutoSum button. Other functions can be quickly added by selecting the cell in which

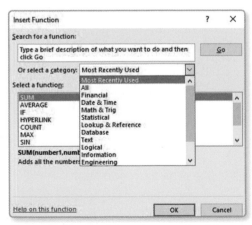

Above: The Function dialogue box separates all the functions into different categories to make them easier to find.

Above: In Excel 2000 and earlier, Functions can be entered into a cell by clicking on the Paste Function toolbar button, which has the letters fx displayed on it.

the function should be displayed, then clicking on the fx toolbar button in Excel 2000 or earlier versions, or clicking on the fx button in the formula bar (above the column letters) in later versions.

Choosing a Function

After clicking on the fx button on the formula bar or toolbar (depending on which version of Excel you are using), a dialogue box will

Hot Tip

There's no need to start a function with an = symbol. Just click on the fx button.

appear with a list of functions. The functions are grouped by category, displayed on the left or via a drop-down list. A definition of each appears in the dialogue box when you select it.

Hot Tip

In Excel 2002 and later versions there is a search box inside the Insert Function dialogue box, so you can enter the name of a function and look for it.

Filling in Function Boxes

After choosing a particular function from the list, click on OK and the dialogue box will display one or more white boxes in which to enter the details of the function. Cell references or ranges can be typed into these boxes, or the cells selected and the ranges will be automatically entered. Excel guides you through the creation of the function, displaying instant error messages if the criterion is incorrect. If the criterion is correctly entered, the result of the function will be displayed inside the dialogue box.

Above: Excel guides you through the process of entering function criteria, and displays results or error messages where appropriate.

WRITING A FUNCTION

It is possible to write a function, and many people prefer this method to using the function dialogue box. Excel versions 2007–2016 provide on-screen guidance when writing a function, showing the criteria that need to be entered. Just like any other calculation, functions must start with an = symbol. Writing a function can result in more mistakes than using the dialogue box, however. Some functions, for

Hot Tip

An old function can be edited by selecting its cell and clicking on the fx button.

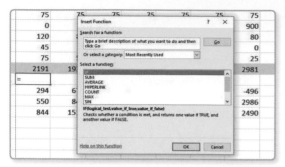

Above: The IF function can sometimes be found within the Most Recently Used category of the function dialogue box – otherwise, look in the Logical category.

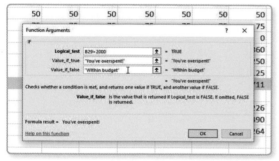

Above: An IF function consists of three parts: a question, such as 'Is the grand total greater than 2000?', followed by an answer if right and an answer if wrong.

19	Car insurance		120	120	120	120	120	120
20	Petrol		125	125	125	125	125	125
21	Car tax		0	0	0	0	0	0
22	Food		500	500	500	500	500	500
23	Clothes		50	50	50	50	50	50
24	Eating out + T/ways		75	75	75	75	75	75
25	Holidays		0	0	0	0	0	0
26	Cash withdrawn		120	80	250	160	180	130
27	Repairs		45	0	0	0	0	0
28	Misc		75	56	63	52	45	12
29	Total Expenses		2191	1937	2114	2188	2201	2118
30	Monthly budget=£2000	You've overspent!						+
31	Surplus/Deficit		294	673	371	297	284	517
32	Opening Balance		550	844	1517	1888	2185	2469
33	Closing Balance		844	1517	1888	2185	2469	2986

Above: A function can be copied down or across to other cells in a table or list and the cell references will be automatically changed.

example, use commas and brackets; these are automatically entered when using the dialogue box, but not when a function is written. If these are omitted, the function will not work.

STEP-BY-STEP: CHECK SPENDING WITH IF

The IF function is useful for comparing or checking figures and displaying warning messages or calculations. The following step-by-step guide shows how to create a simple monthly budget and display an error message if spending exceeds a certain amount.

1   Either download the sample file, or create a table of expenses, with months across the top and expense types down the left side of the screen. Add AutoSum (Σ) totals along the bottom of the table and to the right.

2   Select an empty cell below the first grand total for the first month of the table. This can be used to display an error message if the grand total is above a specific amount (i.e., if too much has been spent).

3   Click on the fx button on the formula bar or the toolbar. A function dialogue box will appear. IF might be listed underneath the

Most Recently Used category. If not, change the category to Logical and find it in the alphabetically sorted list of functions. Select the IF function from the list and click on OK.

4   The IF function offers three white boxes in which to enter criteria. The first box (Logical Test) is like a question. In this case, the question concerns whether the grand total is above £2,000. Click inside the white box for the Logical Test, then select the cell for the respective grand total and type >2000.

5   Click inside the middle white box, labelled Value if True. Type the text 'Spent too much'. This message will be displayed if the grand total is more than 2,000. Next, click in the third white box, labelled Value if False. This box can display a message if the grand total is less than 2,000, so type 'Underspent' in here.

6   The function dialogue box will instantly display a result for the IF function that has been created, so you can see if a mistake has been identified. If the result displayed in the dialogue box looks correct, click on the OK button to close the box.

7   Copy the IF function across the screen using AutoFill. To do this, select the cell containing the IF function, hover the mouse pointer over the bottom right corner of the cell until it changes to a small black cross, then hold the left button down and move to the right across the other cells in which the function should be applied (the cell references will be automatically changed).

Hot Tip

A blank message can be displayed for a Value if True/False by entering double speech marks with a space between, like this: " "

Hot Tip

When entering text into the Value if True/False boxes for an IF function, Excel automatically inserts double speech marks around the words.

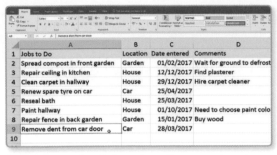

	A	B	C	D
1	Jobs to Do	Location	Date entered	Comments
2	Spread compost in front garden	Garden	01/02/2017	Wait for ground to defrost
3	Repair ceiling in kitchen	House	12/12/2017	Find plasterer
4	Clean carpet in hallway	House	29/12/2017	Hire carpet cleaner
5	Renew spare tyre on car	Car	25/04/2017	
6	Reseal bath	House	25/03/2017	
7	Paint hallway	House	01/10/2017	Need to choose paint colo
8	Repair fence in back garden	Garden	15/01/2017	Buy wood
9	Remove dent from car door	Car	28/03/2017	
10				

Above: Create a list of jobs to do, making sure each one has a date; this can be used to find jobs that are overdue by 60 days, for example.

Above: Enter the current date in a cell by typing =Now() – the format of the date might be wrong, so open the Format Cells dialogue box to change it.

Above: The IF function can compare two cells and in this example, calculate a difference between two dates.

STEP-BY-STEP: FIND OVERDUE DATES WITH IF AND NOW()

Excel can be used to list or highlight date-related information, such as overdue invoices or incompleted jobs. The following step-by-step guide uses a list of jobs and calculates the number of days that have passed since the job was entered. If the number of days exceeds a certain amount, a warning message appears.

1   Using a new Excel workbook, enter a simple list of jobs to do, as shown in the illustrations. Make sure a date is entered for each job, indicating when the job first arose.

2   Scroll across the screen and select cell G1. We're going to enter a function here to display the current date. Type the words =Now(). Press Return and the current date will be displayed, but its format may be wrong. Right click inside the cell, choose Format Cells and a dialogue box will appear. Select the Number tab in the dialogue box, choose Date from the list on the left and select a suitable date type from the list on the right. Click on OK to close the dialogue box.

3   Add a new heading to the list called Overdue (in the illustrations, this heading is entered

into cell E1). Select the cell below it (E2 in our example). This is where the first IF function will be entered to determine whether the job on that row is more than 60 days overdue. The IF function will calculate the difference between the current date and the date the job arose, and display a message accordingly.

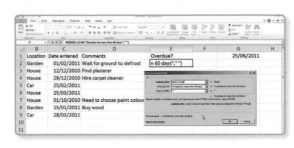

Above: The IF function calculates the difference between the current date and the date of the job, if it's more than 60 days, a warning message will be displayed.

4   Click on the fx toolbar or formula bar button and a function dialogue box will appear. Look for the IF function In the Most Recently Used category or the Logical category. Select the IF function from the list and click on OK. The three parts to the IF function will be displayed.

Above: A function can be copied down or across to other cells in a table or list.

5   Click inside the first white box for the Logical Test of the IF function. We are going to ask whether the difference between the current date and the date of the job is more than 60 days. Type the criterion G1-C2>60. Cell C2 contains the date of the first job (change it if not).

6   Enter the text you want to be displayed if the IF question is true (e.g. if it is overdue by more than 60 days) and if it's false (enter double speech marks with a blank space between to display no comment). Click on OK when finished.

7   Copy the IF function down the job list using AutoFill. To do this, select the cell containing the IF function, hover the mouse pointer over the bottom right corner of the cell until it changes to a small black cross, then hold down the left button and move down to copy the function (the cell references will be automatically changed).

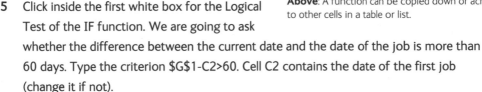

COMBINING FUNCTIONS

A function can be used within a function. For example, an IF function can check whether a cell exceeds a particular value, and if it does, a second IF function can check whether the amount it exceeds is greater than 1,000 (i.e., critical). This is also useful for outstanding invoices – any due date that is beyond 90 days can be found with one IF function, but the second IF function can check the value of the invoice and display a message to write it off if it is below a specific value.

Nesting IF Functions

When two or more IF functions are used in the same calculation it is known as nesting IF functions. A second IF function has to be added to the Value if True or Value if False boxes when the first IF function is being created. Adding a second IF function can be tricky, but the following sections explain how to do it.

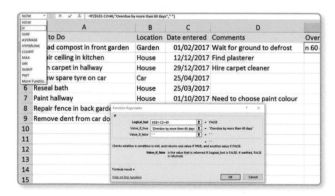

Above: Functions within functions can be added in Excel 97 and later versions by clicking on the drop-down list shown here (only displayed when the Function dialogue box is open).

Nesting IF Functions (pre-97)

In very early versions of Excel, there is a small fx button next to the Value if True and Value if False boxes. Click on one of these to add a second IF function.

Nesting IF Functions (97–2016)

When creating the first IF function using the function dialogue box, complete as much of it as possible, then click inside the white box for the Value if True/False where the second IF function needs to be entered. Look at the top left corner of the screen, above column A. There will be a drop-down triangle to the left of the cross, a tick on the formula bar and a function displayed next to it. If the IF function is displayed here, click on it to start a second IF. Otherwise, click on the drop-down triangle and choose it from the list.

Using Two or More Functions

Different functions can be added within a function in the same way as nesting IF functions. In Excel 97 to 2016, use the drop-down list near the top left corner of the screen to add another function. In earlier versions of Excel, click on the fx button next to the part of the function where it needs to be added.

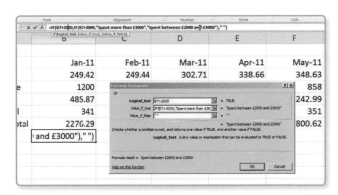

Hot Tip

It often helps to draw a flow diagram for multiple IF functions, so you can see where the path of Value if True/False conditions leads to.

EDITING OLD FUNCTIONS

An old function can easily be edited by selecting the cell in which it is displayed and clicking on the fx button on the toolbar or formula bar. The functions dialogue box will open, displaying the function or one of the functions contained in the selected cell.

Above: Two or more functions together can look confusing, but open the Functions dialogue box and click along the calculation in the formula bar to move to different sections of it.

MOVING BETWEEN FUNCTIONS IN A CELL

When creating or editing a cell containing two or more functions, it can be difficult to ensure the result is correct. Excel can help, thanks to the function dialogue box and the formula bar. With the dialogue box open on screen, displaying the criteria for one of the functions, look at the formula bar above the column headings. The entire calculation for the cell will be displayed. Move to any of the functions in this calculation by clicking on the relevant section on the formula bar. The functions dialogue box will change accordingly.

USEFUL FUNCTIONS FOR LOANS AND INVESTMENTS

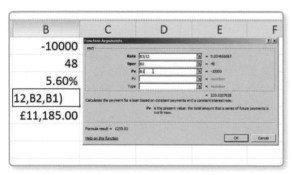

Above: The PMT function can be used to calculate the repayments for a loan based on a fixed interest rate.

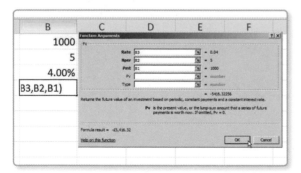

Above: The FV function can be used to calculate the final figure for a regular investment.

Excel has some useful functions that can help with financial planning, including borrowing and investing money.

Calculate a Loan using PMT

The PMT function can be used to calculate how much monthly repayments will be on a loan. Just enter the amount to borrow, the number of repayments and the interest rate, and Excel's PMT function will do the hard work. The illustration here shows how the PMT function can be created in the functions dialogue box. Note that the amount borrowed in cell B1 is -10,000 and the interest rate is divided by 12 to allow it to be calculated on a monthly basis (assuming the repayments are monthly). The calculation for Total repaid in cell B5 is =B4*B2.

See Regular Investments Grow with FV

The FV (future value) function calculates the final figure on regular investments based on a fixed interest rate. This is useful for seeing how much an annual investment of £1,000 per year over five years will be worth at the end of the term, for example. The FV function is similar to the PMT function for loans. The result is a negative value, but can easily be reversed by displaying the sum invested as a negative value instead.

Lump-Sum Investments with FV

Finding the final value of a lump-sum investment can also be calculated in Excel using the FV function. The criterion is a little different to using the FV function for a regular annual or monthly investment, though. A zero value has to be entered in the PMT box when creating this function

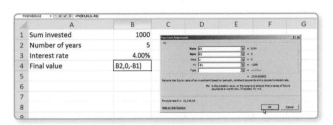

Above: The end value of a lump-sum investment can be calculated using the FV function.

and the FV box contains the lump-sum amount. The result is a negative value, but can be reversed in the same way as above – by changing the sum invested to a negative amount.

TIDYING UP TEXT WITH FUNCTIONS

Information in Excel is often displayed in a table or list format in columns or rows of uniform structure. There is very little room for writing sentences to summarize or interpret the data, so information can sometimes be difficult to understand. However, Excel's text functions can tidy up the text in cells and combine it to help summarize or explain information.

Combine Cells with &

The contents of several cells can be combined and displayed in one cell using the & symbol (hold down the Shift key on the keyboard and press the number 7). This is useful

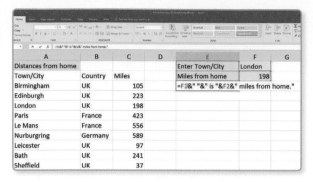

	A	B	C	D	E	F	G
	Distances from home				Enter Town/City	London	
	Town/City	Country	Miles		Miles from home	198	
	Birmingham	UK	105		=F1&" "&" "is "&F2&" miles from home."		
	Edinburgh	UK	223				
	London	UK	198				
	Paris	France	423				
	Le Mans	France	556				
	Nurburgring	Germany	589				
	Leicester	UK	97				
	Bath	UK	241				
	Sheffield	UK	37				

Above: Cell contents can be combined to create meaningful sentences from data; each cell reference or piece of text is separated with an & symbol.

> ## Hot Tip
> Excel has a function called Concatenate, which is the same as using & symbols to combine cells.

for summarizing data from a table and performing calculations with meaningful text alongside. Choose an empty cell to display the combined text and start with an = sign. Select a cell to include its contents and type the text in double speech marks. Separate each cell reference or piece of text with an & symbol.

Left and Right Trimming

Sometimes the text in a cell is too long, especially with downloaded bank statements or other downloaded data. The two functions called Left and Right can help. Left, for example, displays a specific number of characters in a cell, starting at the left-hand side. Right does the opposite. So, a column of long descriptions can be trimmed by replacing it with a separate column with only 10 characters, for example. The first column can then be hidden.

B	C
Transaction	
NAWAAB KHAN RESTAU LEEDS	NAWAAB KHA
CASH SAINSBY OCT31 SAIN - MATLO@14:08	CASH SAINS
INTERNAL TRANSFER	INTERNAL T
MCDONALDS REST. SCARBOROUGH	MCDONALDS
PIZZA HUT 155 SCARBOROUGH	PIZZA HUT
MOUNTAIN WAREHOUSE SCARBOROUGH	=LEFT(B7,10)
CASH NATWEST OCT27 N/RAIL LEEDS@13:43	LEFT(text, [num_chars])
TESCO STORE 2808 LEEDS	
TESCO STORES SACAT LEEDS	
FIRST GREATWESTERN	
	100202

Above: The Left function can be used to display only a specific number of characters from a cell, starting at the left-hand side.

Other Useful Text-Tidying Functions

The last section of this chapter includes a list of functions and their definitions. Look at the list of text functions for more suggestions. Text functions including Upper, Trim and Clean are all useful for tidying up text in a spreadsheet.

VLOOKUP FUNCTION

The Vlookup function is one of the most popular but confusing functions in Excel. It is useful for finding unique information in a long list, such as a product code, employee ID number or specific date. However, there are some important rules to adhere to when creating a Vlookup to ensure it works correctly.

UNDERSTANDING VLOOKUPS

Vlookup stands for Vertical Lookup. This function is a search method that can retrieve and display information from a list. By entering a word, code or date in a cell, a Vlookup can use this information and find it in a list, then retrieve and display any data from adjacent columns in the list.

Vlookup Examples

➔ **Product code updates:** Downloaded sales data can be summarized and tidied using several Vlookup functions. These can be used to find the latest results for a set of product codes or names.

Above: In this Vlookup example, a town/city can be entered in cell F1 and the Vlookup in cell F2 will find the mileage from the list on the left.

➔ **Employee details:** Specific information from a long list of employees' details can be retrieved by entering an employee's unique ID number and using Vlookup to find it.

➔ **Discounts:** A Vlookup doesn't always have to find a specific value. If a range of discounts are available, depending on how much is spent (e.g. 10% for over £100 and 15% for over £300), then a Vlookup can find the nearest match and provide a discount value.

Vlookup Rules

The following checklist will ensure you create a Vlookup function that works correctly and reliably.

➔ **List down**: A Vlookup searches down a list for a piece of unique information, so make sure the data to be searched is displayed as a list.

➔ **Avoid blanks**: Make sure the list of data is all together, with no blank rows.

Hot Tip

If a list runs across the screen instead of down it, use the Hlookup (Horizontal Lookup) function instead of the Vlookup (Vertical Lookup).

➔ **First column**: The first column in the list will be searched down using Vlookup, so this column needs to contain the relevant data.

➔ **Unique or nearest match**: Vlookup can only be asked to search for a unique entry in a list. Otherwise, it will find the first or nearest match and display the result. In some cases, a nearest match is useful (e.g. different discounts for total price based on a lookup value).

Vlookup Parts

There four sections of criteria to complete when creating a Vlookup using the function dialogue box.

➔ **Lookup value**: This is the data that will be used to search down a list and find the exact match or nearest match in the first column.

Function Arguments ? X

VLOOKUP

Lookup_value		= any
Table_array		= number
Col_index_num		= number
Range_lookup		= logical

=

Looks for a value in the leftmost column of a table, and then returns a value in the same row from a column you specify. By default, the table must be sorted in an ascending order.

Lookup_value is the value to be found in the first column of the table, and can be a value, a reference, or a text string.

Formula result =

Help on this function   OK   Cancel

Right: The Vlookup consists of four criteria, which can be difficult to understand at first.

➔ **Table array:** This is a range of cells (list), down which Vlookup will search to find an exact or nearest match based on the Lookup value. Vlookup will search down the first column, starting at the top.

➔ **Column index number:** Once Vlookup has found a match in the list for the Lookup value (nearest match or exact), then the column index number specifies how many columns to the right the Vlookup must move before retrieving the information in a cell. The first column in the list is number 1.

➔ **Range lookup:** This determines whether the Vlookup should find an exact match (e.g. a product code or name) or a nearest match (e.g. price ranges with discount percentages). Enter the word False to find an exact match, or leave blank to find the nearest match. This is one aspect of a Vlookup where mistakes are often made.

STEP-BY-STEP: CREATING A VLOOKUP

The following step-by-step guide shows how to create a list of towns or cities with a corresponding list of distances to these places from home. To save time on scrolling up and down the list to search for a particular town or city, a destination can be entered in a separate cell and a Vlookup used to find that place in the list and display the mileage.

1   Enter a list of town and city names in column A, a corresponding list of countries in column B and the approximate distance from home to these places in column C. This table/list will be used by a Vlookup to find a particular town or city.

2   Enter the headings shown in the illustration for cells E1 and E2, then enter a town or city name from the table or list in cell F1. The data in cell F1 will be used by Vlookup to locate the relevant information in the list/table.

3   Select cell F2, where the Vlookup will be located. Click on the fx button on the formula

bar or toolbar (depending on the version of Excel). Vlookup may be listed in the dialogue box that appears, but if it isn't, change the Category to Lookup & Reference and scroll down the function list to find Vlookup (it's sorted alphabetically). Once selected, click on OK.

Above: In this example, the search data will be displayed in cell F1 and the Vlookup will be created in cell F2.

4   Click inside the first white box, labelled Lookup value, and select cell F1. Click inside the second white box (Table array) and select the cells containing the names of the cities/ towns, countries and miles. Click inside the third white box (Col index num) and type the number 3 (for the third column in the table). Finally, click in the last white box and type the word False (this will ensure an exact match is found).

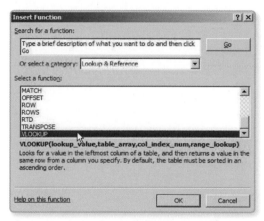

Above: The Vlookup function is listed under the Lookup & Reference category within the function dialogue box.

5   After entering data in all four boxes, a result will be displayed in the dialogue box. If it's wrong, check the details entered and make sure the town/city entered in F1 is spelt correctly. Click on OK to close the dialogue box. Test the Vlookup by changing the town/city name in cell F1.

Above: Entering the word 'false' in the Range lookup section of a Vlookup ensures only an exact match is found in a table/list.

FUNCTIONS DEFINED

There are thousands of different functions in Excel. The following pages define the most useful and explain their functions. They are divided into types of function for ease of reference.

DATABASE FUNCTIONS

The database functions, known collectively as the DFunctions, are used to analyze data that forms part of a list or database. To use these functions, data needs to be entered so that Excel recognizes it as a list or database.

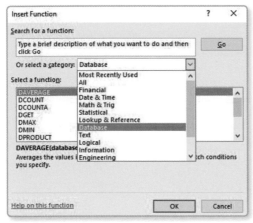

Above: The database functions in Excel can be found within the Database category of the functions dialogue box.

DAVERAGE(database,field,criteria)

Calculates the average of the values in a column based on the conditions specified.

DCOUNT(database,field,criteria)

Counts the number of cells containing numbers in a column based on the conditions specified.

DCOUNTA(database,field,criteria)

Counts all the cells in a column that are not blank based on the conditions specified.

Above: The DAverage function in this example can calculate the average mileage for a country, based on the country displayed in cell E6.

DGET(database,field,criteria)
Extracts a single value from a column based on the conditions specified.

DMAX(database,field,criteria)
Returns the largest (maximum) number in a column based on the conditions specified.

DMIN(database,field,criteria)
Returns the smallest (minimum) number in a column based on the conditions specified.

DSUM(database,field,criteria)
Adds (sums) the numbers in a column based on the conditions specified.

DATE AND TIME FUNCTIONS

Date and time functions can extract date and time values from cells in a worksheet, displaying full or part information. They also provide tools for analyzing and calculating date and time values.

DATE(year,month,day)
Displays the serial number of a given date.

DATEVALUE(date_text)
Converts a date represented by text to a serial number.

Hot Tip

Database functions are used to extract or calculate data in a list, so make sure the data is correctly presented first.

DAY(serial_number)
Displays the day of the month as an integer ranging from 1 to 31.

DAYS360(start_date,end_date,method)
Designed for accountants working on a 360-day year (12 30-day months), this function provides the number of days between two given dates.

EDATE(start_date,months)
Returns the serial number for the date that is a specified number of months before or after a given date (start date).

EOMONTH(start_date,months)
Returns the serial number for the last day of the month that is a specified number of months before or after the start date.

HOUR(serial_number)
Displays the hour as an integer (ranging from 0 [12 a.m.] to 23 [11 p.m.]), based on the given serial number.

MINUTE(serial_number)

Displays the minute as an integer (ranging from 0 to 59) based on the given serial number.

MONTH(serial_number)

Returns the month as an integer (ranging from 1 [January] to 12 [December]), based on the given serial number.

Above: The Month function displays the month as a number based on a date from another cell.

NETWORKDAYS
(start_date,end_date,holidays)

Displays the number of whole working days between the given start and end date (excludes weekends and any dates identified as holidays).

NOW( )

Displays the serial number of the current date and time (based on the computer's clock).

Above: The NetworkDays function is useful for calculating the number working days spent on a project because it ignores weekends.

SECOND(serial_number)

Returns the second as an integer (ranging from 0 to 59), based on a given serial number.

TIME(hour,minute,second)

Returns the serial number of a particular time as a decimal fraction ranging from 0 to 0.99999999.

TIMEVALUE(time_text)

Converts a time represented as text into a serial number.

TODAY( )

Returns the serial number of the current date.

WEEKDAY(serial_number,return_type)

Returns the day of the week as an integer (ranging from 1 [Sunday] to 7 [Saturday]).

B	C	D	E	F
Start date	End Date	Days worked	Est days	Est End
04/08/2017	07/08/2017	2	2	
08/08/2017			11	23/08/2017

Above: The Workday function is useful for calculating the length of time project work will take, based on a working week; using a start date and estimated number of days, it calculates an end date and ignores weekends.

WORKDAY(start_date,days,holidays)
Returns the serial number of a date that is a given number of working days before or after the start date (excludes weekends and any dates identified as holidays).

YEAR(serial_number)
Displays the year as an integer (ranging from 1900 to 9999), based on a given serial number.

YEARFRAC(start_date,end_date,basis)
Calculates the fraction of the year based on the number of whole days between two given dates.

FINANCIAL FUNCTIONS
Financial functions perform popular business calculations, often those related to borrowing or saving money. Most of these functions can be found in the Financial category in the function dialogue box.

ACCRINT(issue,first_interest,settlement ,rate,par,frequency,basis)
Returns the accrued interest based on a security paying periodic interest.

ACCRINTM(issue,maturity,rate,par,basis)
Returns the accrued interest for a security paying interest at maturity.

DB(cost,salvage,life,period,month)
Returns the depreciation of an asset for a specified period (uses the fixed-declining balance method).

DDB(cost,salvage,life,period,factor)
Returns the depreciation of an asset for a specified period using the double-declining

Hot Tip
When searching down the alphabetically sorted function list in the function dialogue box, jump to a function by pressing the first letter of it on the keyboard.

balance method or some other method you specify.

EFFECT(nominal_rate,npery)
Returns the effective annual interest rate, given the nominal annual interest rate and the number of compounding periods per year.

FV(rate,nper,pmt,pv,type)
Returns the future value of an investment based on periodic, constant payments and a constant interest rate. Can also be used to calculate the future value of a lump-sum investment.

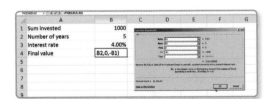

Above: The FV function can be used to calculate the final value of a lump sum investment.

FVSCHEDULE(principal,schedule)
Calculates the future value of an investment with a variable or adjustable rate.

INTRATE(settlement,maturity, investment,redemption,basis)
Returns the interest rate for a fully invested security.

IPMT(rate,per,nper,pv,fv,type)
Returns the interest payment for a given period for an investment based on periodic, constant payments and a constant interest rate.

IRR(values,guess)
Returns the internal rate of return for a series of cash flows represented by the numbers in values.

NOMINAL(effect_rate,npery)
Returns the nominal annual interest rate, given the effective rate and the number of compounding periods per year.

NPER(rate,pmt,pv,fv,type)
Returns the number of periods for an investment based on periodic, constant payments and a constant interest rate.

NPV(rate,value1,value2,...)
Calculates the net present value of an investment by using a discount rate and a series of future payments (negative values) and income (positive values).

PMT(rate,nper,pv,fv,type)
Calculates the payment for a loan based on constant payments and a constant interest rate.

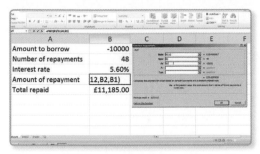

Above: The PMT function can be used to calculate the repayments for a loan based on a fixed interest rate.

PPMT(rate,per,nper,pv,fv,type)

Returns the payment on the principal for a given period for an investment based on periodic, constant payments and a constant interest rate.

PV(rate,nper,pmt,fv,type)

Returns the present value of an investment.

RATE(nper,pmt,pv,fv,type,guess)

Returns the interest rate per period of an annuity.

SLN(cost,salvage,life)

Returns the straight-line depreciation of an asset for one period.

SYD(cost,salvage,life,per)

Returns the sum-of-years' digits depreciation of an asset for a specified period.

VDB(cost,salvage,life,start_period, end_period,factor, no_switch)

The variable declining balance function calculates the depreciation of an asset for any given period.

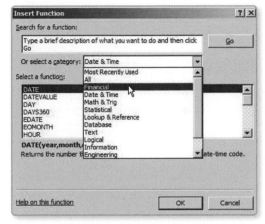

Above: The financial functions in Excel have their own category within the function dialogue box.

Hot Tip

Some financial functions display a negative result, but this can be changed to a positive by adding a minus symbol in front of one of the cell references when creating the function.

INFORMATION FUNCTIONS

Information functions provide status information about a selected cell. The majority of information functions are referred to collectively as the IS functions. They can be used to check the type of value and return TRUE or FALSE depending on the outcome.

CELL(info_type,reference)

Provides details of formatting, location or contents of the selected cell or worksheet.

Above: The Cell function can be used to retrieve data about a cell or the workbook itself – the function =Cell("filename"), for example, displays the location where the Excel file is saved.

COUNTBLANK(range)

Counts empty cells in a given range of cells. Useful for finding missing information in downloaded data.

ERROR.TYPE(error_val)

Returns a number representing an Excel error value.

INFO(type_text)

Provides information on the current operating environment. For example, =INFO("Release") displays the version of Excel in use.

ISBLANK(value), ISERR(value), ISERROR (value), ISLOGICAL(value), ISNA(value), ISNONTEXT(value), ISNUMBER(value), ISREF(value), ISTEXT(value)

Each of these nine functions, referred to collectively as the IS functions, checks the type of value and returns TRUE or FALSE depending on the outcome.

ISEVEN(number)

Returns TRUE for an even number and FALSE for an odd number.

ISODD(number)

Returns TRUE for an odd number and FALSE for an even number.

N(value)

Converts a value to a number. Useful for downloaded data where cells containing numbers don't seem to work when used in a calculation.

NA( )

Returns the error #N/A, (no value is available).

TYPE(value)

Indicates type of value (i.e., number, text). Useful for checking downloaded data.

Above: The Type function is useful for checking downloaded data to make sure it's in the correct format; the example here reveals that the adjacent cell is a number, whereas the other cells are text (the Type function uses number codes).

LOGICAL FUNCTIONS

The logic or conditional functions are used to test whether a specified condition is true or false. This is Excel's way of asking a question about the contents or value of a cell. These functions are often combined with other functions.

AND(logical1,logical2,...)

Returns TRUE if all its arguments are TRUE; returns FALSE if one or more arguments is FALSE.

FALSE( )

Returns the logical value FALSE.

IF(logical_test,value_if_true,value _if_false)

One of the most popular logical functions. Returns one value if a condition you specify evaluates to TRUE and another value if it evaluates to FALSE. Use IF to conduct conditional tests on values and formulas.

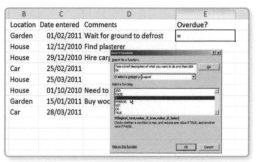

Above: One of the most popular logical functions is IF; this has many uses, including error checking and finding unpaid and overdue invoices.

NOT(logical)

Reverses the value of its argument. Use NOT when you want to make sure a value is not equal to one particular value.

OR(logical1,logical2,...)

Returns TRUE if any argument is TRUE; returns FALSE if all arguments are FALSE.

TRUE( )

Returns the logical value TRUE.

LOOKUP AND REFERENCE FUNCTIONS

The Lookup and Reference functions provide the facility to locate a specific value from a list or find a reference for a specific cell.

ADDRESS(row_num,column_num,abs _num,a1,sheet_text)

Generates a cell address as text, using the given row and column numbers.

AREAS(reference)

Returns the number of areas (a range of contiguous cells or a single cell) in a reference.

CHOOSE(index_num,value1,value2,...)

Selects one of up to 29 values based on the given index number.

COLUMN(reference)

Returns the column number of the given reference.

COLUMNS(array)

Returns the number of columns in an array or reference.

HLOOKUP(lookup_value,table_array ,row_index_num,range_lookup)

Searches for a value in the top row of a table and returns a value in the same column from a row you specify in the table or array.

HYPERLINK(link_location,friendly _name)

Creates a shortcut or jump that opens a document stored on a network server, an intranet or the internet.

INDEX(array,row_num,column_num) or (reference,row_num,column_num, area_num)

Returns the value of a specified cell or array of cells within an array or reference. Useful for picking data from a single list.

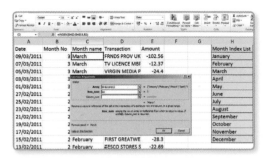

Above: In this example, the Month function in column B extracts a month number from column A; the Index function is then used in column C to find the month number in the list on the right (in yellow) and consequently display the name of the month.

INDIRECT(ref_text,a1)

Displays the reference specified by a text string. Used to change the reference to a cell within a formula without changing the actual formula.

LOOKUP(vector) and LOOKUP(array)

The vector form of LOOKUP looks in a one-row or one-column range for a value and returns a value from the same position in a second one-row or one-column range. The array form of LOOKUP looks in the first row or column of an array for the specified value and returns a value from the same position in the last row or column of the array.

MATCH(lookup_value,lookup_array, match_type)

Locates the relative position of an item in an array that matches a specified value in a specified order.

OFFSET(reference,rows,cols,height,width)

Returns a reference to a range that is a specified number of rows and columns from a given cell or range of cells.

ROW(reference)

Displays the row number for a given reference.

ROWS(array)

Calculates the number of rows in a given reference or array.

Above: The Rows function can be used in a downloaded bank statement to find the number of transactions made over a particular period, because it counts the number of rows in a range of cells.

TRANSPOSE(LINEST(Yvalues,Xvalues)) and TRANSPOSE(array)

Transposes a vertical range of cells to a horizontal range, or vice versa.

VLOOKUP(lookup_value,table_array,col _index_num,range_lookup)

Searches for a value in the leftmost column of a table, and returns a value in the same row from a column you specify in the table.

Above: Vlookup is one of the most popular functions. It's useful for extracting data from a long list and is covered more in depth in this chapter.

MATHS FUNCTIONS

The range of maths functions provides the facility to perform both simple and complex mathematical calculations.

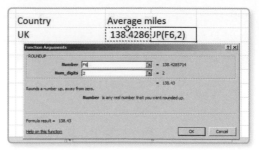

Above: The Round functions, including Roundup and Rounddown, are used to tidy up numbers and reduce the risk of incorrect values.

COUNTIF(range,criteria)
Counts the number of cells in a given range based on a specified criteria.

PI( )
Returns the number 3.14159265358979, accurate to 15 digits.

PRODUCT(number1,number2, ...)
Multiplies all the given numbers and returns the product.

RAND( )
Returns a random number greater than or equal to 0 and less than 1. A new random number is returned every time the worksheet is calculated.

RANDBETWEEN(bottom,top)
Returns a random number between the specified numbers. A new random number is returned every time the worksheet is calculated. Useful for quickly creating sample data to test.

ROUND(number,num_digits)
Rounds a number to a specified number of digits; ROUND(2.75,1) equals 2.8.

ROUNDDOWN(number,num_digits)
Rounds a number down, toward zero; ROUNDDOWN(6.2,0) equals 6.

ROUNDUP(number,num_digits)
Rounds a number up, away from zero; ROUNDUP (6.2,0) equals 7.

SIGN(number)
Determines the sign of a number (1 for a positive number, 0 if the number is 0 and -1 if the number is negative).

SQRT(number)
Returns the square root of a positive number; SQRT(16) equals 4.

SUM(number1,number2, ...)

Adds all the numbers in a range of cells; SUM(3,2,6) equals 11.

SUMIF(range,criteria,sum_range)

Adds the cells that meet a specified criteria.

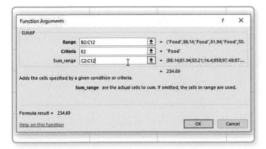

Above: The SumIf function can add up specific transactions in a bank statement, such as salary payments, as long as the transaction description remains the same.

SUMPRODUCT(array1,array2,array3,...)

Multiplies corresponding components in the given arrays, and returns the sum of those products.

STATISTICAL FUNCTIONS

Excel provides numerous statistical functions, from the most commonly used SUM and AVERAGE functions through to the cumulative beta probability density function. Some of the functions are designed for specialist use, but many prove useful in everyday worksheets.

AVEDEV(number1,number2,...)

Returns the average of the absolute deviations of data points from their mean.

AVERAGE(number1,number2,...)

Returns the average (arithmetic mean) of the given numbers.

BETADIST(x,alpha,beta,A,B)

Returns the cumulative beta probability density function, commonly used to study variation in a percentage across samples, such as the fraction of the day people spend driving.

CONFIDENCE(alpha,standard_dev,size)

Determines, with a particular level of confidence, a range on either side of a sample mean. For example, if you drive to work each day, the earliest and latest you will arrive.

CORREL(array1,array2)

Uses the correlation coefficient to determine the relationship between two properties – for example, the relationship between the temperature and ice-cream sales.

COUNT(value1,value2,...)

Counts all the values that are numbers. If the value is a cell address, Excel will check whether the cell contains a number and, if so, include it in the count.

COUNTA(value1,value2,...)

Counts the number of cells in a range that are not empty.

FORECAST(x,known_y's,known_x's)

Calculates or predicts a future value by using existing values; used to predict future sales, inventory requirements or consumer trends.

MAX(number1,number2,...)

Returns the largest (maximum) number in the range.

MAXA(value1,value2,...)

Returns the largest value in a list of arguments. Text and logical values such as TRUE and FALSE are compared as well as numbers.

MEDIAN(number1,number2,...)

Returns the median – the number in the middle of a set of given numbers; half the numbers have values that are greater than the median, and half have values that are less.

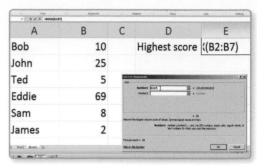

Above: Statistical functions, including Max, Min, Average, Median and Mode, can all be used to analyse a list of results.

MIN(number1,number2, ...)

Returns the smallest (minimum) number in the range.

MINA(value1,value2,...)

Returns the smallest value in the list of arguments. Text and logical values such as TRUE and FALSE are compared, as well as numbers.

Above: The Rank function can analyse a list of results and display a value that shows the position of each value amongst all the other results.

MODE(number1,number2,...)

Returns the most frequently occurring, or repetitive, value in a range of data.

RANK(number,ref,order)

Returns the rank (size relative to other values) of a number in a list of numbers. If the list is sorted, the rank of a number is its position in the list.

TEXT FUNCTIONS

Text functions allow cells to be combined, trimmed and calculated to help eliminate unwanted data and make a spreadsheet easier to understand.

CHAR(number)

Displays the character that represents the given number.

CLEAN(text)

Removes all the non-printable characters from the specified text. Used to remove characters that will not print when importing data from another application.

CONCATENATE (text1,text2,...)

Joins several cells and pieces of text

together to form a single text string inside one cell.

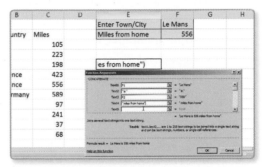

Above: The Concatenate function can be used to combine data in cells with additional text to help summarize and make sense of results.

EXACT(text1,text2)

Compares two text strings and returns TRUE if they are exactly the same and FALSE if they differ. EXACT is case-sensitive but ignores formatting differences. Useful for importing the latest sales results into a spreadsheet with existing results.

FIND(find_text,within_text,start_num)

Finds specific text from within other text. The starting position of the text found is displayed as a number representing the position from the leftmost character of the text string. For example, =FIND("smith","john smith") will return 6.

This function is similar to SEARCH, but FIND is case-sensitive and does not allow wildcard characters.

FIXED(number,decimals,no_commas)
Rounds a number to a specified number of decimal places, formats the number in decimal format using a period and commas, and returns the result as text.

LEFT(text,num_chars)
Returns the first (or leftmost) character or characters in a cell.

LEN(text)
Returns the number of characters in a cell.

LOWER(text)
Converts all upper-case letters in a cell to lower-case.

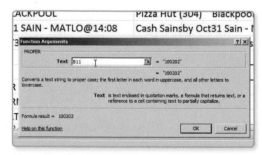

Above: Text functions, including Upper, Lower and Proper, can be used to change the case of text (e.g. all capitals or all lower case).

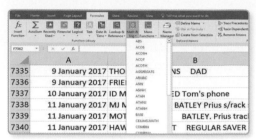

Above: In Excel 2007–2016, most of the formulas can be found by clicking on the Formulas ribbon tab and using the buttons along the top of the screen.

MID(text,start_num,num_chars)
Returns a given number of characters from a cell, starting at the position specified.

PROPER(text)
Capitalizes the first letter in a cell and any other letters that follow any character other than a letter. Converts all other letters to lower-case letters.

REPLACE(old_text,start_num,num _chars,new_text)
Replaces part of a text string with a different text string.

REPT(text,number_times)
Repeats text a given number of times.

RIGHT(text,num_chars)
Returns the last (or rightmost) character or characters in a cell.

SEARCH(find_text,within_text,start_num)

Locates a character or text string within another text string returning the number of the character at which a specific character or text string is first found, reading from left to right.

SUBSTITUTE(text,old_text,new_text,instance_num)

Substitutes new text for old text in a cell.

TEXT(value,format_text)

Converts a value to text using a specific number format.

TRIM(text)

Removes all spaces from text except for single spaces between words. Used to trim spaces from text received from another application that may have irregular spacing.

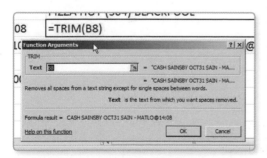

Above: Downloaded data can often include too many spaces between text in a cell, so the Trim function can remove these and help reduce the width of the columns.

UPPER(text)

Converts text to uppercase.

VALUE(text)

Converts a text that represents a number to a number.

FORECASTS, REPORTS AND PRESENTATIONS

FORECASTING

Excel provides some useful tools to help predict future sales, expenditure results and similar figures. The following section shows how to assess forecasts for cash flows, profit and loss, and investments.

MULTIPLE FORECASTS WITH SCENARIO MANAGER

Scenario Manager can display different values in a spreadsheet. If these values are used in a calculation, a variety of forecasts can be produced. This has many uses – from speculating on an investment with different interest rates to examining a cash-flow forecast with different levels of expenses and income.

Hot Tip

Scenario Manager is useful for changing values used in calculations.

Finding Scenario Manager (pre-2007)

Click on the Tools menu and choose Scenarios. The Scenario Manager dialogue box will appear on screen. If it is not displayed on the Tools menu, click on the double arrows at the bottom of the menu to expand it.

Finding Scenario Manager (2007–2016)

Click on the Data ribbon tab and select the What-If Analysis button near the top right of the screen. A short menu will drop down. Select Scenario Manager from this list and a Scenario Manager dialogue box will appear on screen.

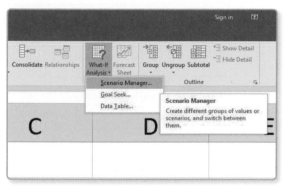

Above: Scenario Manager in Excel 2007–2016 can be found by clicking on the Data ribbon tab and selecting the What-If Analysis button.

Adding Scenarios to One Cell

With the Scenario Manager dialogue box open, decide on which cell to change (make sure it's not a calculation, as it will be deleted). Click on the Add button and an Add Scenario dialogue box will appear. Enter a name for this scenario (e.g. Low_figures), then click inside the Changing cells box and select the cell to change. Click on OK and a Scenario Values dialogue box will appear. Enter a value for the selected cell to change, then click on Add to continue creating more scenarios. Repeat this instruction as many times as necessary.

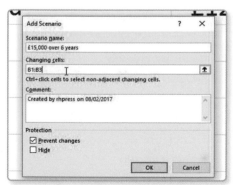

Above: Enter a name for the scenario and choose a cell to change – make sure this is not a cell containing a calculation because it will be overwritten.

Adding Scenarios to More than One Cell

When selecting cells to change (inside the Add Scenario dialogue box), hold down the Ctrl key

on the keyboard and click inside all the cells to be changed. They will in turn be added to the Changing cells box. Click on OK and a list of all the cells to change will appear, whereby different values can be entered.

Above: Multiple cells can be changed using the Scenario Values function.

Showing Scenarios

After entering two or more Scenarios, return to the Scenario Manger dialogue box, where all of the scenarios will be listed. Select one from the list, then click on the Show button. The cell values on screen will change, along with any related calculations.

Editing Scenarios

If a scenario is wrong – for example, if the cell values change to the wrong amounts or do not change at all – then it can be amended in the following way:

- Make sure the Scenario Manager dialogue box is displayed
- Select the scenario to amend and click on the Edit button
- The Add Scenario dialogue box will appear, in which the cells to change can be altered
- Click on OK to open the Scenario Values dialogue box, where the cell values can be amended
- Click on OK to complete editing the scenario
- Test the scenario by selecting it from the list and clicking on the Show button

Hot Tip

Scenarios can be removed from the list in the Scenario Manager dialogue box by selecting one and clicking on the Delete button.

Producing a Scenario Summary

A summary of all the scenarios and subsequent results can be displayed as a table or PivotTable in the following way:

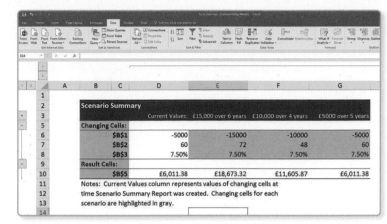

Above: Scenarios can be summarized to display all the different forecast values and results.

- Click on the Summary button in the Scenario Manager dialogue box
- Choose between a Scenario Summary or a Scenario PivotTable
- Make sure the cell reference in the Result cells box is the cell containing the calculation that changes when the different scenarios are applied
- Click on OK
- A summary or PivotTable will be displayed on a new worksheet

ASKING EXCEL TO FIND THE ANSWER

Excel's Goal Seek can be used to find out the value required to produce a specific result. For example, if you want to invest some money for 10 years with a fixed interest rate of five per cent, you may want to know how much to invest to ensure the final amount is worth £15,000. Goal Seek can calculate this.

Using Goal Seek

Select a cell containing a calculation. In Excel 2007–2016, click on the Data ribbon tab, select the What-If Analysis button and choose Goal Seek from

Hot Tip

Goal Seek has to use a calculation and can only change one cell.

B	C
13585.962	
5	
2.00%	
£15,000.00	

Above: Goal Seek can be used to see how the result of a calculation can be created by changing one of the cells that affects it.

the menu that drops down. In earlier versions of Excel, click on the Tools menu and choose Goal Seek. From the dialogue box that appears, make sure the Set cell box displays the cell reference containing a calculation. Enter a value in the middle box (the result you want). Click inside the bottom box and select a cell. This can be changed and in turn will alter the calculation (e.g. the amount to be invested). Click on OK and Goal Seek will display an answer.

ADDING DROP-DOWN VARIABLES

Drop-down lists with different numbers can be added to a spreadsheet to help with forecasting. An investment spreadsheet can have drop-down lists for different investment amounts, terms (years) and interest rates. This feature is also useful for forecasting cash flows with drop-down lists for a range of expense amounts, income and other variables.

Creating the Values

When creating drop-down values, the list of variables to be used in a particular cell must be displayed inside the spreadsheet. For example, if a varying number of years needs to be used in an investment forecast, create a list of numbers in the spreadsheet.

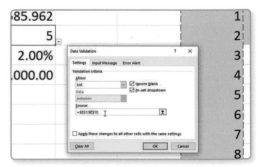

Above: Data Validation can be used to create drop-down variables for forecasting.

Creating a Drop-Down List

With a list of numbers displayed elsewhere in the spreadsheet, select the cell to which the drop-down list will apply. In Excel 2007–2016, click on the Data ribbon tab and select the Data Validation button. In earlier versions of Excel,

Hot Tip

Use a drop-down list to change a number that affects a calculation.

click on the Data menu and choose Validation. From the dialogue box that appears, make sure the Settings tab is selected. Choose List from the drop-down beneath Allow. Click inside the Source box, then select the cells containing the list of numbers. Click on OK to close the dialogue box.

Using a Drop-Down List

Once you have created a drop-down list, a drop-down triangle should be displayed to the right of the cell the list was created for. Click on it and a list will appear. Select an item from the list and the cell's contents will change. If this cell is used in a calculation, then the result of the calculation will change.

STEP-BY-STEP: MAKING A CASH-FLOW FORECAST

The following step-by-step guide shows how to create a cash-flow forecast for household income and expenditure.

1   Open Excel and, with a new file on screen, save it (hold down the Ctrl key and press S) as Cashflow. Double-click on the sheet tab that opens at the bottom of the screen and rename it to the year for the cash flow (e.g. 2011).

2   Select cell B1 and enter the starting month for the cash flow. Reselect the cell, position the mouse pointer over the bottom right corner of the cell, and when it changes to a small black cross, hold the left button down. Move across the screen to create a sequence of months.

3   Enter the word Income in cell A2, then list some sources of income and enter the words Total Income at the bottom of this list (see illustration on page 184). Enter some income

amounts underneath the months across the screen. Apply some fill colours to the cells where appropriate.

4 Select all the income cells and the empty row for Total Income. Click on the AutoSum toolbar button (Σ), which is in the Home ribbon tab in Excel 2007–2016 and the Standard toolbar in earlier versions. The totals will be automatically applied to the Total Income row.

5 Enter a heading for Expenses in column A, below the income section, then list a number of typical expenses (mortgage, utility bills, petrol, food). Enter some values for these expenses underneath the months. Create a Total Expenses row and use AutoSum to add up each month's expenses.

6 Scroll down to the area below the expenses. Enter the words Surplus/Deficit in an empty cell in column A, then the words Opening Balance below, and finally Closing Balance.

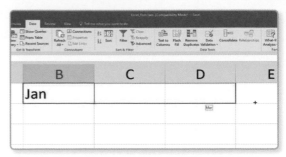

Above: Use Autofill to create a sequence of months.

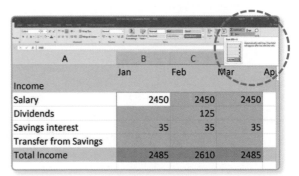

Above: Select all of the income value cells, plus the row where the total income figures will be displayed, then click on the AutoSum button to insert income totals automatically.

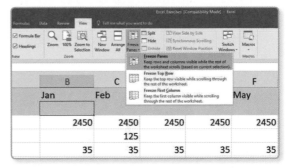

Above: Select cell B2 and freeze the panes to keep the headings on screen when scrolling; in Excel pre-2007, click on the Window menu to Freeze Panes.

7 Select the first Surplus/Deficit cell for the first month (in column B). This cell will contain a calculation that works out the difference between the month's total income and total expenses. Press = on the keyboard to start a calculation, then select the Total Income cell in column B, press – (minus symbol) on the keyboard and select the Total Expenses cell in column B. Press Enter/Return. Use AutoFill to copy the calculation across the screen.

VLOOKUP	X ✓ fx =B7-B29		
	A	B	C
1		Jan	Feb
23	Clothes	50	
24	Eating out + T/ways	75	
25	Holidays	0	
26	Cash withdrawn	120	
27	Repairs	45	
28	Misc	75	
29	Total Expenses	⊕ 2191	19
30			
31	Surplus/Deficit	=B7-B29	
32	Opening Balance		
33	Closing Balance		

Above: The Surplus/Deficit calculation subtracts Total Expenses from Total Income.

8 Enter an amount for the opening balance for the first month. Select the cell for the Closing Balance in column B. Create a calculation that adds the Surplus/Deficit and the Opening Balance. Copy it across using AutoFill (the figures will be incorrect at this time).

VLOOKUP	X ✓ fx =B33		
	A	B	C
1		Jan	Feb	Ma
26	Cash withdrawn	120	80
27	Repairs	45	0
28	Misc	75	56
29	Total Expenses	2191	1937
30			
31	Surplus/Deficit	294	673
32	Opening Balance	550	=B33
33	Closing Balance	⊕ 844	673

Above: After the first month, the Opening Balance is the previous month's Closing Balance.

9 Select the Opening Balance for the next month in column C. This is last month's Closing Balance, so press = and select last month's Closing Balance. Press Enter, then copy the calculation across the screen using AutoFill.

Hot Tip

Select cell B2 and freeze the panes to ensure the months and Income/Expenses remain on screen when scrolling.

PRODUCING REPORTS

Reports need to summarize data and present it in a format that is clear and easy to understand. Excel has a variety of features that help produce professional-looking reports that offer accessible information.

REPORTING ON A BANK STATEMENT

A downloaded bank statement can be difficult to understand, especially if it consists of hundreds – perhaps thousands – of transactions. However, there are a number of tools in Excel to help extract specific analytical information.

Total Interest on a Mortgage

If a downloaded bank statement lists mortgage payments in and negative values for interest charges, then a SumIf function can add up all the interest payments. In this case, the SumIf

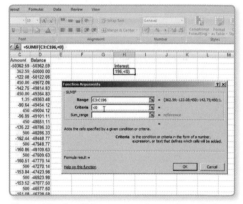

Above: The SumIf function can be used to calculate numbers in a range of cells which are above or below a specified amount.

works because it only adds up numbers less than zero. This is a simple function to set up, requiring only the column containing amounts to be selected and the criterion <0 to be entered.

STEP-BY-STEP: CALCULATE TOTAL MONTHLY SPENDING

The DSum function can be used to calculate all negative values (spending) between two dates in a bank statement, so a summary figure or series of summary figures can be displayed to show spending patterns. The criteria for the DSum need to be displayed on screen and the following step-by-step guide shows how to do this.

1   Make sure the downloaded bank statement is a list and has headings across the top for Date and Amount. Enter the Date heading twice in two blank cells and enter a start date underneath one of them with a > symbol at the beginning. Enter an end date beneath the other Date heading with a < symbol at the beginning of the date. This sets the criteria for the date range.

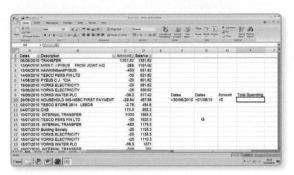

Above: Enter the criteria for the DSum in the spreadsheet, making sure that the criteria headings match the list headings.

2   Enter a heading for Amount and type <0 beneath it (all negative values will be added). It is good practice to keep all the Date and Amount headings together as a small table (see the illustration as a guide). Select another empty cell to display the DSum. Click on the fx button on the toolbar or formula bar.

Above: DSum consists of three parts: a list, a column to add up, and criteria.

3   With the function dialogue box open, change the category to Database and find DSUM in the list. Select it and click on OK. A DSUM dialogue box will appear with three white boxes. Click inside the white box for Database. Select the cells in the list, including the headings at the top.

4   Click inside the white box for Field. Select the cell containing the Amount heading in the list. Finally, click in the Criteria white box and select the criteria cells (including the headings, dates and values) that were created in steps 1 and 2. A Formula result will be displayed inside the DSUM dialogue box. If it's wrong, check the cell references, otherwise click on OK.

CONSOLIDATING DATA

Large volumes of data are often easier to understand if they are separated into months or quarters and displayed on separate worksheets. However, when it comes to bringing all that data together and displaying grand totals, it can be time-consuming. Fortunately, there is a useful tool in Excel called Data Consolidation, which can total data across worksheets and workbooks.

Hot Tip

Select a group of sheets where the tabs are all together by clicking on the far left/right sheet tab, holding down the Shift key on the keyboard and clicking on the sheet tab at the opposite end.

Data Structure

Data Consolidation works more effectively across several spreadsheets if the structure of the data is the same. This ensures Excel can pick the same figures from each spreadsheet and add up each one to produce summary totals. It helps, therefore, to create a number of worksheets that all have the same structure. This can be done quickly by grouping sheets (selecting a group of them), so that whatever is typed into one sheet is also typed into the other grouped sheets. Hours of typing and copying can be saved using this method.

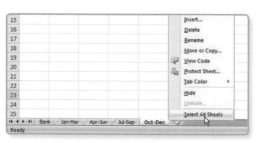

Above: Grouping worksheets can save hours of repetitive typing and copying.

Grouping Sheets

All the worksheets in an Excel workbook can be grouped at once by right-clicking on a sheet tab and choosing Select All Sheets. All the sheet tabs will be highlighted and whatever is typed into one will be

Hot Tip

Rename a worksheet
by double clicking on its
sheet tab.

	A	B	C	D	E	F
1	Expense Type	Oct	Nov	Dec	Totals	
2	Council Tax	120	120	120	360	
3	Electricity	75	75	75	225	
4	Water	90	90	90	270	
5	Gas	65	65	65	195	
6	Home insurance	25	25	25	75	
7	Car loan	156	156	156	468	
8	Car tax	22	22	22	66	
9	Car insurance	57	57	57	171	
10	Totals	610	610	610	1830	
11						

Above: The utility and other bills listed in the quarterly worksheets can be totalled in the Year Totals sheet using Data Consolidation.

typed into all of them. If only a few of the sheets need grouping (not all of them), hold down the Ctrl key on the keyboard and click on the sheet tabs that need grouping to select them. To ungroup the sheets, right-click on a sheet tab and select Ungroup Sheets.

Creating a Consolidation Worksheet

The illustration on this page for Data Consolidation shows a workbook containing quarterly worksheets with utility and other bills. A separate Year Totals sheet is created, which will contain all the totals for the different bills. Data Consolidation will take the total values from each worksheet, add them up and display a grand total in the Year Totals sheet. Before proceeding, it's worthwhile copying the headings for the bills over to the Year Totals sheet.

Above: Data Consolidation allows cells from other worksheets to be added into a grand total calculation.

Hot Tip

Insert extra worksheets in Excel 2007–2016
by clicking on the button to the right of
the sheet tabs (it has a small + symbol). In
earlier versions of Excel, click on the Insert
menu and choose Worksheet.

Activating Data Consolidation

Select the cell inside the worksheet in which you want the consolidated totals to be displayed (the Year Totals sheet in our example). Click on the Data menu or ribbon tab and select the Consolidate button or menu option, depending on the version of Excel.

Completing the Data Consolidation Dialogue Box

→ **Make sure the Sum function is displayed in the top box of the Consolidate dialogue box**

→ **Click inside the white box for Reference**

→ **Click on the first sheet tab containing the values to consolidate**

→ **Select the relevant cells (the totals in our example)**

→ **Click on the Add button in the Consolidate dialogue box**

→ **Repeat this process for the other worksheets**

→ **Click on OK to see the grand totals displayed**

Hot Tip

Row and column labels/headings can be included in a Data Consolidation. Look for the tick boxes in the Consolidate dialogue box.

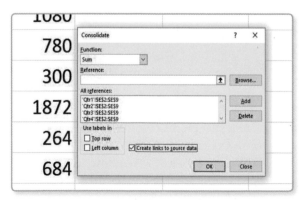

Above: Add a tick mark to the option labelled 'Create links to source data', and the consolidated totals will be kept up to date.

Create Links to Source Data

Data Consolidation is useful for summarizing large amounts of data and producing a grand total. The totals will not be updated unless the option labelled 'Create links to source data' is ticked. If this option is ticked, the totals will be updated. Also, all the figures used to calculate the totals will be displayed – click on the Outline buttons down the left side of the screen or the number buttons near the top left corner to see the values.

PRESENTING EXCEL DATA

Excel is often used in presentations or the data from it is utilized in other programs. For this reason, the information needs to be professionally presented. As always, Excel can help you create impressive presentations.

CREATING CHARTS

Data presented in a chart format is often easier to understand and trends are easier to spot. Excel has an extensive range of chart tools, but all these options mean that a chart can take a long time to create. The following section reveals the shortcuts and quick techniques to making an effective and professional-looking chart.

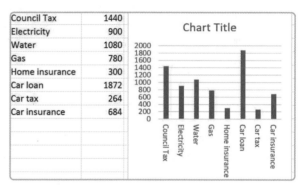

Above: In Excel 2007–2016, you can display a chart next to the selected cells.

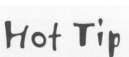

Chart data should ideally be displayed in a table format with headings or labels across the top or down the left side (or both). This makes it easier for Excel to understand the structure of the data and produce a chart from it.

Press F11 or Alt+F1

One of the quickest methods for creating a chart is to select the cells that need to be included in the chart (including any headings or labels) and press F11 on the keyboard. A chart will be instantly created and displayed in a separate worksheet. In Excel 2007–2016, pressing Alt and F1 will display a chart next to the selected cells (in earlier versions it displays a chart in a separate sheet).

Changing the Chart Type

The type of chart can be quickly changed by right-clicking inside a space in the Chart and choosing Change Chart Type or Chart Type (depending on the version of Excel). From the dialogue box that appears, there will be a number of different types of charts listed and within each type, there will be a choice of styles – including 3D and 2D. In later versions of Excel, once a chart has been selected, there will be a number of options displayed across the top of the screen to enable it to be changed and altered.

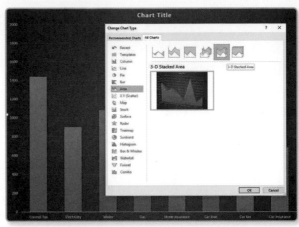

Above: Changing chart type is a quick task.

MANIPULATING CHARTS

Once you have your chart set up, there are several ways of manipulating the data contained within it.

Changing Chart Colours

The colour of just about anything in a chart can be changed. Right-click on the part of the chart to change and choose Format Data Series (or a similar option beginning with the word Format)

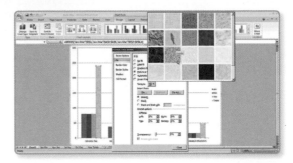

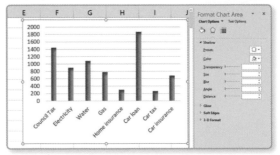

Above: The colour of any object can be changed in a chart by right clicking on that object and choosing Format Data Series to open a dialogue box or a pane on the right of the screen.

from the shortcut menu that appears. A
dialogue box will appear on screen. Click
on the tabs along the top (pre-2007
Excel) or options down the left side
(Excel 2007–2010) to look for different
colours and patterns. In later versions of
Excel, there are options across the top
of the screen and down the right side to
enable the chart to be altered.

Move a Chart

A chart created on a separate sheet
can be displayed next to the data
it represents. Right-click around the
perimeter of the chart, inside a
space. From the shortcut menu
that appears, select Location or
Move Chart (right-click elsewhere
if these options are not displayed).
A small dialogue box will appear
with the option to place the chart
in an existing worksheet.

A chart displayed next to its data
can be moved using the drag-and-
drop method. Hover the mouse in
a space around the perimeter of
the chart, then hold down the left
button and move the mouse to
move the chart.

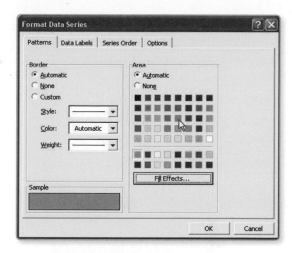

Above: Pre-2007 versions of Excel use a straightforward
Format Data Series dialogue box to enable the colour of
any part of a chart to be modified.

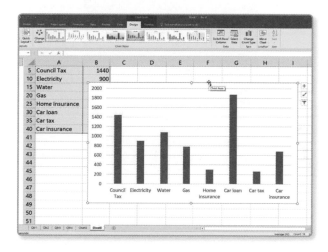

Above: A chart displayed next to its data can be moved using the
drag-and-drop method: hover the mouse in a space around the
perimeter of the chart, then hold the left button down and move the
mouse to move the chart.

Add More Data

If an extra row or column of data needs to be added into a chart, right-click around the perimeter of the chart in a space and choose Source Data or Select Data. From the dialogue box that appears, change the cell references for the chart to include more data.

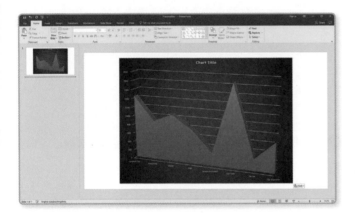

Copying a Chart to Another Program

A chart created in Excel can be copied into a presentation program such as Microsoft PowerPoint or into a report within Microsoft Word. The easiest way to do this is to click once inside the chart to select it, then hold the Ctrl key down on the keyboard and press C to copy it. In Excel 2003 and earlier versions, a series of dotted lines will appear around the chart. Open the program and file to copy the chart into. Right-click where you want the chart to be positioned and choose Paste from the shortcut menu. The chart should appear.

Above: A chart can be copied from Excel into a presentation program such as Microsoft PowerPoint or a report in Word.

ILLUSTRATING EXCEL

Excel can not only help you create professional-looking charts for presentations – data can also be enhanced with diagrams to highlight important sections, as well as photographs and illustrations to produce a professional finish.

DRAWING TOOLS

Excel and other Microsoft Office programs use a set of drawing tools, which are useful in Excel for highlighting cells and making notes on the worksheet.

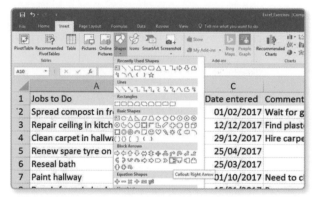

Using Drawing Tools (pre-2007)

A Drawing toolbar is usually displayed along the bottom of the screen. If this is not visible, right-click on any toolbar button and choose Drawing from the menu that appears. Click on the arrow, line, box or oval

Above. The drawing tools in Excel include arrows and text boxes to help highlight cells and make notes on them.

buttons to draw these shapes (move into the spreadsheet, hold down the left button and move the mouse). A wider range of drawing shapes can be found on the AutoShapes button.

Using Drawing Tools (2007–2016)

Click on the Insert ribbon tab and look at the Illustrations section of the ribbon near the top left corner of the screen. Click on the Shapes button and a large palette of

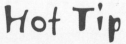

Arrows, lines and other objects can be moved by selecting them, then using the arrow keys on the keyboard.

Above: You can add text to most drawn objects by right-clicking inside them.

groups of shapes will appear, ranging from arrows and lines to boxes and stars. Select one from the list, then move into the worksheet and left-click to draw the shape.

Creating Text Boxes

Most large shapes drawn in Excel can have text displayed inside them. After drawing the object, right-click inside it and choose Edit Text or Add Text. A flashing cursor will appear. Type the text, then click elsewhere to finish.

Resizing Drawn Objects

A drawn object can be resized by selecting it, then hovering the mouse pointer over any of the small squares or circles around it. When the mouse pointer changes to a double-headed arrow, hold down the left button and move the mouse to resize the object.

Rotating a Drawn Object

In Excel 2000 and earlier versions, select an object and click on the Rotate button (this looks like an arrow in the shape of a circle) on the Drawing toolbar. A series of green circles will appear around the object. In later versions of Excel, one circle will appear above the object after selecting it. In all cases, position the mouse pointer over the circle and when it changes to an arrow in the shape of a circle, hold down the left button and move the mouse to rotate the object.

Creating Process Flow Diagrams

The range of block arrows and other symbols within Excel's drawing tools means diagrams such as process flow charts can be created to help

Hot Tip

Use Connectors to link between shapes. These lines automatically connect or snap to shapes, making it easier to draw flow diagrams.

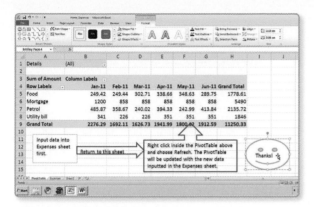

Above: Process flow diagrams can be used to illustrate a step-by-step guide to using a spreadsheet.

illustrate data and explain how to use the spreadsheet. For example, a process flow chart could illustrate how to input data into a spreadsheet and update a PivotTable. In Excel 2003 and earlier versions, block arrows and similar shapes are on the AutoShapes button of the Drawing toolbar. In Excel 2007–2016, click on the Insert ribbon tab and choose the Shapes button.

Grouping Shapes

A diagram consisting of several shapes can be difficult to move around the screen. However, if all the shapes are grouped together they can be easily moved together. To group shapes:

- **Select one of them**
- **Hold down the Shift key on the keyboard and select all the other shapes**
- **Right-click on one of them**
- **Choose Group or Grouping**
- **Select Group from the sub-menu**
- **Try moving one of the shapes – all of them will move**

To ungroup the shapes:

- **Right-click on any shape**
- **Choose Group/Grouping**
- **Select Ungroup from the sub-menu**

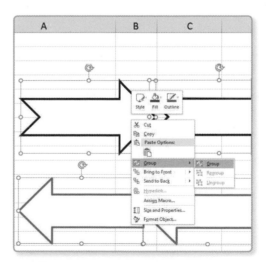

Above: Grouping shapes and lines enables them to be moved together as one object.

Left: WordArt in Excel 2003 and earlier versions is chosen and written using two dialogue boxes before it is displayed in the worksheet.

WORDART

WordArt can help produce some professional-looking titles for a spreadsheet and enhance the presentation of data.

Using WordArt (pre-2007)

WordArt in Excel 2003 and earlier versions is inserted by clicking on the WordArt toolbar button on the Drawing toolbar (it looks like a blue letter A on an angle). A WordArt dialogue box will appear; choose a style of WordArt and click on OK. Type the text for the WordArt and click on OK. The WordArt will appear on the worksheet and can be moved, rotated and resized, just like a shape.

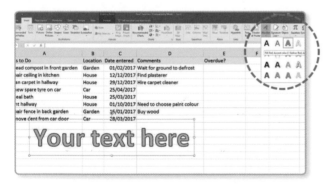

Above: WordArt in Excel 2007–2016 is created by clicking on the Insert ribbon tab and selecting the WordArt button.

Using WordArt (2007–2016)

Click on the Insert ribbon tab and select the WordArt button near the top right of the screen. A palette of WordArt styles will drop down. Choose one and a sample WordArt will appear on screen with the words 'Your text here'. Click inside these words, delete them and type your own words. The WordArt can be moved, rotated and resized, just like a shape.

CLIPART, PICTURES AND PHOTOS

Clipart images and photographs can transform a spreadsheet into a professional presentation, with company logos and colourful backgrounds. In Excel 2013/2016, ClipArt is known as Pictures.

Hot Tip

Click on the Insert menu in Excel 2003 and earlier versions, choose Picture and select WordArt.

Library Clipart and Pictures

Excel makes use of a Microsoft Office ClipArt library, which contains an assortment of illustrations. These can be accessed in Excel 2003 and earlier versions by clicking on the Insert menu, choosing Picture and selecting ClipArt from the sub-menu. Either a dialogue box or a ClipArt task pane on the right side (Excel 2002–2003) will appear. In Excel 2007/2010, click on the Insert ribbon tab and select the ClipArt button. A ClipArt task pane will appear on the right side of the screen. In Excel 2013/2016, click on the Insert ribbon tab, select Online Pictures, and a search box will appear.

Searching for ClipArt and Pictures

The Online Pictures, ClipArt dialogue box or task pane can be used to search for online pictures or ClipArt (such as money) by typing a keyword in the search box. Excel will display any relevant images. To add a Picture or ClipArt to a spreadsheet, select the image then either double-click on it, click on Insert, or drag and drop it on to the worksheet. The image can then be resized and moved.

Above: Search for ClipArt/Pictures by entering a keyword, such as 'money', 'accounting', 'cash' or 'people'.

LOGOS, PHOTOS AND COMMERCIAL IMAGES

Images that are not listed in the ClipArt library can be inserted. In Excel 2003 and earlier versions, click on the Insert menu, choose Picture and Select From File. In Excel 2007–2016, click on the Insert ribbon tab and select the button labelled Picture (near the top left corner of the screen). In all cases, an Insert Picture dialogue box will appear, similar to the dialogue box for opening an Excel file. Locate a picture, then click on the Insert button. The picture will be added as an object to the worksheet and can then be resized and moved.

Using a Logo or Photo for a Worksheet Background

Inserting ClipArt and other images into a spreadsheet is useful for livening it up with additional illustrations, but if the images are too large they will get in the way of the data. Add an illustration as a background, however, and the picture acts as a fill colour for the cells, so data can be displayed over the top of it.

A background should ideally consist of an image that is either very light so dark text can be displayed over it, or very dark so that bright white or yellow text can be displayed over it.

Hot Tip

Search the internet for free-to-use images, which can be saved to your computer and used in your Excel presentations.

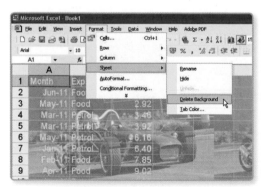

Above: Backgrounds can sometimes make it difficult to read the data inside the cells, so try to use images that are faint with light colours.

Inserting a Background (pre-2007)

To insert a background in versions of Excel before 2007, take the following steps:

- ⤷ **Click on the Format menu and choose Sheet**
- ⤷ **Select Background from the sub-menu. A dialogue box will appear**
- ⤷ **Locate a suitable picture file, then click on Open or Insert**

The background image will be added to the worksheet on screen and will be tiled (repeated several times). If the image is too big or too light/dark, it will need to be edited in a program such as Microsoft Paint or a photo-editing package, then inserted again.

Inserting a Background (2007–2016)

To insert a background in Excel 2007–2016, take the following steps:

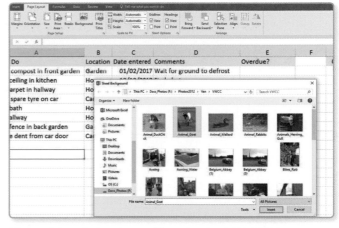

- Click on the Page Layout ribbon tab and select Background
- A Sheet Background dialogue box will appear
- Locate a suitable picture file, then click on Open

Above: Click on the Page Layout ribbon tab in Excel 2007–2016 and select the Background button to add a background image.

The background image will be added to the worksheet on screen and will be tiled (repeated several times). If the image is too big or too light/ dark, it will need to be edited in a program such as Microsoft Paint or a photo-editing package, then inserted again. A background can be removed by returning to the Page Layout ribbon tab and clicking on the Delete Background button.

PRINTING EXCEL DATA

Excel spreadsheets can be printed out, but problems can easily arise with too many pages, blank pages and data that is either too big or too small to fit on the printed page. This section reveals the quickest techniques for printing as well as how to resolve typical problems.

Above: The Print Preview screen shows how each page will be printed before it's sent to the printer.

PRINTING TRICKS

There are right and wrong ways to print data in Excel, and these are usually only ever discovered when the paper has been ejected from the printer! There are, however, several techniques to help ensure a printout from Excel is correctly laid out.

Check with Print Preview

Before embarking on printing some data in Excel, always check how it will be printed and what it will look like by opening Print Preview. In Excel 2003 and earlier versions, there's a Print Preview button on the Standard toolbar, which looks like a white piece of paper with a magnifying glass. In Excel 2007, click on the Office button at the top left and choose Print, followed by Print Preview. In Excel 2010–2016, click on the File ribbon tab and choose Print. In all cases, a preview of how the Excel worksheet will be printed is displayed on screen.

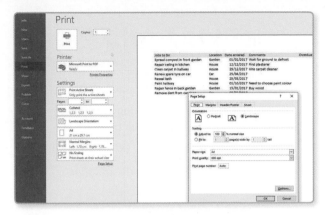

Hot Tip

In Excel 2007–2016, hold down the Ctrl key on the keyboard and press F2 to open the Print Preview screen.

Check and Change Print Settings

Several print settings can be changed to ensure the data fits on to a single page. Most of the useful options can be found in Excel 2007 and earlier versions by clicking on the Setup or Page Setup button

Above: If you're familiar with the Page Setup dialogue box for printing, it can be opened in Excel 2010–2016 after clicking on the File ribbon tab, selecting Print and choosing Page Setup near the bottom of the screen.

in Print Preview or by clicking on the File menu and choosing Page Setup (Excel 2003 and earlier versions). In Excel 2010–2016, the settings are displayed on screen alongside the print preview, but a Page Setup dialogue box can be opened from here by clicking on this option near the bottom left of the screen.

Landscape to Portrait

Select the Page tab in the Page Setup dialogue box (Excel 2007 and earlier versions) to switch between portrait and landscape. In Excel 2010–2016, Portrait or Landscape Orientation settings are on the left side of the Print Preview screen, or the same Page Setup dialogue box can be opened by clicking on the Page Setup option near the bottom left of the screen.

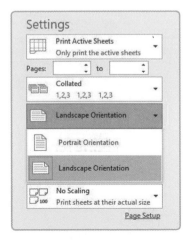

Squeeze It In

The Print Preview screen usually reveals that a table of data will be printed across three pages, when in fact it can be squeezed on to one or two. You can adjust the settings to see if this is possible. From the Page Setup dialogue box (or the Print screen in Excel 2010–2016), select the Page tab, change the scaling settings and click on OK to see if this helps. Excel 2010–2016 has a scaling setting at the bottom left of the print screen, or the traditional Page Setup dialogue box can be used.

Tweak the Margins

The margins (the spaces left at the bottom, top, left and right sides of the page) used by the printer can usually be changed to help squeeze more data on to a page. From the Page Setup dialogue box, click on the Margins tab and change the values in the boxes for Top, Left, Right and Bottom.

Check with Page Break View

Page Break Preview is a spreadsheet view showing how many cells will be printed on each page. This view is activated in Excel 2003 and earlier versions by clicking on the View menu and choosing Page Break Preview (return to this menu and select Normal to switch off Page Break Preview). In Excel 2007–2016, there are small buttons for Normal, Page Layout and Page Break Preview in the bottom right corner of the screen.

Above: Page Break Preview provides a worksheet view of how many cells will be printed on each page; drag the dividing lines to change them.

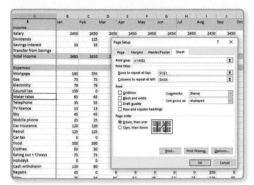

Above: Rows and columns can be repeated on every printed page, which helps with long lists or wide tables with headings or labels.

PRINTING ENHANCEMENTS

There are a number of features in Excel that can enhance the look of a printed spreadsheet and make it look more professional.

Repeat Rows and Columns

When printed, a long list can be difficult to read if the headings at the top are only displayed on the first page. The solution is to repeat a row on every printed page, and the same applies to a wide table – a column of labels can be repeated on every printed page. In Excel 2003 and earlier versions, click on the File menu and choose Page Setup. In Excel 2007–2016, click on the Page Layout ribbon tab and select the Print Titles button. In all cases, the Page Setup dialogue box will appear with the Sheet tab displayed.

Selecting Rows and Columns to Repeat

With the Page Setup dialogue box on screen and the Sheet tab selected, click inside the 'Rows to repeat at top' box for a long list, or click inside the 'Columns to repeat at left', for a wide table. In both cases, select one cell representing the row or column to repeat. The entire row or column will be included in the Page Setup dialogue box. Click on Print Preview to see if the row/column is repeated on every printed page.

Headers and Footers

Information can be printed at the top (header) and bottom (footer) of each page. This is useful if you want to add page numbers, file locations, an author and date. To apply headers and footers:

Above: Headers and footers can be displayed at the top and bottom of each printed page.

- ➲ **Open the Page Setup dialogue box**
- ➲ **Select the Header/Footer tab**
- ➲ **Choose different types of pre-set headers and footers from the drop-down lists or click on the Custom buttons to write your own**

If headers and footers need to be different on the first page or different on odd and even pages (useful when making a book), there are tick boxes for these options (custom headers and footers will need to be created).

Above: Setting the print area makes sure blank pages are not printed.

> ## Hot Tip
>
> A print area can be removed by repeating the steps to set the print area, but choosing Clear Print Area from the sub-menu.

PRINTING PROBLEMS

If too many pages are printed out, you end up with lots of blank pages. Sometimes the quality of the print is very poor; this section will help you troubleshoot and find the solutions.

Blank Pages Printed

If one or more blank pages are printed it means the print area for the worksheet is too large. The easiest way to fix this is to set the print area. Select the cells that need to be printed then, in Excel 2003 and earlier versions, click on the File menu, choose Print Area and select Set Print Area from the sub-menu. In Excel 2007–2016, select the cells to be printed, click on the Page Layout ribbon tab, choose the Print Area button and select Set Print Area from the drop-down menu. In all cases, a solid green or dotted line will appear around the selected cells to indicate the print area.

Leftover Column Printed on a Separate Page

If a column on the far right of a table is printed on a separate page, the scaling and margins need to be changed to make sure it is included with the other columns. Information on how to change these settings can be found on pages 77, 203 and 204.

Row and Column Headings are Printed

If row numbers and column heading letters are printed when you don't want them to be, open the Page Setup dialogue box and click on the Sheet tab. Look for a tick box in the middle of the dialogue box labelled Row and column headings. Remove the tick mark from this option to switch off printing the numbers and letters.

No Gridlines

The gridlines can be switched on and off via the Page Setup dialogue box and the Sheet tab. Look for a tick box labelled Gridlines in the centre of the dialogue box. Add a tick mark to this option to print gridlines, or remove it to ensure gridlines are not printed.

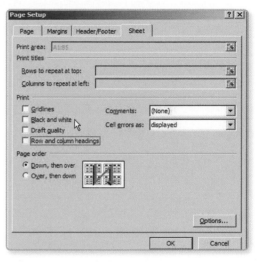

Above: The causes of printing problems can sometimes be found in the Page Setup dialogue box on the Sheet tab.

Poor-quality Print and No Colour

A poor-quality print can sometimes be caused by a draft quality setting in Excel. Open the Page Setup dialogue box and click on the Sheet tab. Look for a tick box in the middle of the dialogue box labelled Draft quality. There is also another option above it labelled Black and white. These options can sometimes be the cause of a poor-quality print (draft quality) and no colours being printed other than black.

Rows or Columns Can't Be Set to Repeat

If you open the Page Setup dialogue box from the Print Preview screen, the settings for repeating rows and columns (on the Sheet tab) cannot be entered. This is because the rows/columns cannot be selected when in Print Preview. Close the dialogue box, return to the normal spreadsheet view and reopen it to set the rows/columns to print on every page.

MISTAKES AND ERRORS

WARNING AND ERROR MESSAGES

Now you've got to grips with many of the functions Excel offers and how to apply them, it's time to find out what to do when things go wrong. Mistakes are easily made, but Excel displays a range of warning and error messages, as well as messages inside cells to help highlight mistakes.

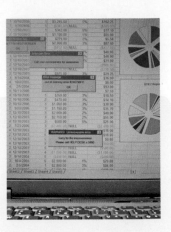

CELL RESULTS ERRORS

If a calculation produces a result such as #N/A or #VALUE?, it means there is a problem with the calculation or the cells to which it refers. Below are some of the common error messages that appear in cells, along with guidance on how to fix the issues.

#NAME?

This means that a cell reference in a calculation is not identified. Check that all cell references are correctly entered in the calculation. If cell names are used, check that all the names can be found by clicking on the Name Box drop-down list near the top left corner of the screen. A list of cell names will appear. Cross-check their spellings with any that are used in the calculation.

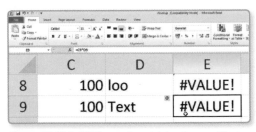

Above: Multiply 100 by a cell containing the word Text or a mistyped entry such as loo (should be 100), and a #VALUE? error will be displayed.

#VALUE?

If an amount displayed in a cell is not a number, date or time, then it cannot be used in a calculation or function. Consequently, a #VALUE? error may

Hot Tip

Result errors such as #N/A and #NUM! can appear in the function dialogue box when creating a function. This immediately warns that there is a problem with part of the function.

appear. This can also occur if a calculation or function refers to a cell containing text. Typing errors may be the cause of such a problem (100 is misread and entered as loo, for example), but imported data can also be misinterpreted, resulting in amounts being displayed as text.

#N/A

This error message can appear in a cell containing a Vlookup function. If the data (lookup value) requested cannot be found by the Vlookup, the 'not available' (#N/A) message is displayed inside the cell. Check the lookup value can be found in the table of data used by the Vlookup. Usually the lookup value has been incorrectly entered.

Above: The #N/A error message is displayed in this Vlookup because the lookup value in cell F1 has been spelt incorrectly and thus cannot be found in the data table to the left.

#REF

If a column, row, worksheet or workbook is referred to in a calculation but has in fact been deleted, the calculation will display the error message #REF. If a calculation refers to cells in another workbook but that workbook has been deleted, renamed or moved, Excel may display a message box offering to help find the workbook and set up a new link to it.

#DIV/0

The #DIV/0 error message appears when a cell has been divided by zero or an empty cell. This type of problem often arises with imported data in which empty cells and rows exist.

Calculations for percentage mark-up in sales figures or percentage sold in stock figures result in #DIV/0 wherever empty cells exist.

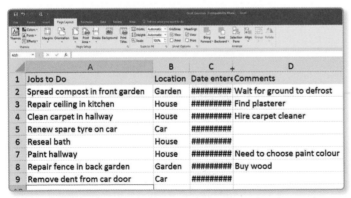

Above: The example here should read =SUM(C2:D5), but instead it reads =SUM(C2 D5).

#NULL!

The #NULL! error is displayed in functions such as SUM, where a cell range has been incorrectly entered and the cells do not intersect. This is usually caused by inaccurately selecting a range of cells to include in a function. Check that the correct range of cells has been selected to resolve this problem.

#NUM!

This error is displayed when a calculation or function contains invalid numeric values.

To fix this, go back and check the values in each of the relevant calculations or functions.

#####

This error usually indicates that a column is not wide enough to display all the characters for a number or date in a cell. This can easily be resolved by widening the column. However, be aware that Excel also displays multiple # symbols if a negative date or time is calculated.

Above: If a cell containing a number or date isn't wide enough the value will be displayed as a series of # symbols.

Knock-on Errors

One error can sometimes be the result of another. If a function or calculation in a cell refers to a cell containing an error message, then this cell will also display an error message. It may take some time to trace the error back to its cause.

CELL WARNING MESSAGES

As well as cell error messages, Excel also has a series of warning messages to alert you to potential problems and help you find a way of avoiding them. Below are some of the most common warning messages you will see when working in Excel.

Circular References

When a calculation includes a reference to the cell containing the calculation itself, it causes an error known as a circular reference. This may consist of several cells leading back to the calculation cell. Fortunately, Excel displays a warning box when it identifies a circular reference and inserts arrows on the screen pointing to the cells that are causing the problem.

Clothes	50	50	50	50	50	50
Eating out + T/ways	75	75	75	75	75	75
Holidays	0	0	0	0	0	0
Cash withdrawn	120	80	250	160	180	130
Repairs	45	0	0	0	0	0
Misc	75	56	63	52	45	12
Total Expenses	2191	1937	2114	2188	2201	2118
Surplus/Deficit	294	673	371	297	284	517
Opening Balance	aza	#####	####	#####	#VALUE!	#VALUE!
Closing Balance	#VALUE!	#####	####	#####	#VALUE!	#VALUE!

Above: The text in cell B31 has had a knock-on effect for the calculation below it and the adjacent calculations in these two rows.

	E	F	G
	Enter Town/City	Loondonn	
	Miles from home	#N/A	
	#N/A		

Value Not Available Error
Help on this error
Trace Error
Ignore Error
Edit in Formula Bar
Error Checking Options...

Above: In Excel 2002 and later versions, a green triangle appears in the top left corner of a cell when an error is identified. Select the cell and a yellow exclamation mark may appear, which can be clicked on to see further help and information.

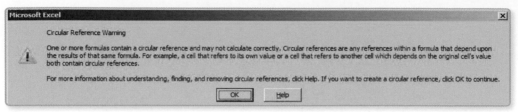

Above: A warning message appears whenever a calculation in a cell refers back to itself; this is known as a circular reference.

Error Indicators

Excel 2002 and later versions display a green triangle or error indicator in the top left corner of a cell when a problem is identified. For more information on the problem, select the cell and an exclamation mark inside a yellow diamond will appear next to the cell. Hover the mouse pointer over the exclamation mark and a short message will appear, explaining the problem. The issue can sometimes be fixed by clicking on the exclamation mark and choosing one of the options from the menu that drops down.

Missing Numbers

One of the most useful cases in which an error indicator appears is in Sum functions for lists of numbers. If a cell is accidentally omitted from the calculation, Excel displays an error indicator that allows you to amend the function. If such an error occurs:

	A	B	C	
14	Water rates	65	65	
15	Telephone	35	35	
16	TV licence	13	13	
17	Sky	45	45	
18	Mobile phone	25	25	
19	Car insurance	120	120	1
20	Petrol	125	125	1
21	Car tax	0	0	
22	Food	500	500	5
23	Clothes	50	50	
24	Eating out + T/ways	75	75	
25	Holidays	0	0	
26	Cash withdrawn	120	80	2
27	Repairs	45	0	
28	Misc	75	56	
29	Total Expenses	1521	1937	21
30	Surplus/Deficit		3	3
31	Opening Balance		4	21
32	Closing Balance		7	25
33				
34				

B29 — =SUM(B11:B27)

Menu options: Formula Omits Adjacent Cells / Update Formula to Include Cells / Help on this error / Ignore Error / Edit in Formula Bar / Error Checking Options...

Above: In this example, the SUM calculation includes cells B15 to B27, but excludes B14 and B28, so Excel displays an error indicator and a message outlining the problem.

- Select the cell in question
- Click on the yellow exclamation mark
- A drop-down menu will be displayed
- From the drop-down menu, select Update Formula to Include Cells
- The Sum function will be amended to include the missing cell

WRONG WARNINGS

Excel can sometimes wrongly identify errors. As an example, take a list of values with a date at the top of the list. If the list is totalled using the Sum function, Excel may display a warning message advising that the date at the top of the list hasn't been included in the calculation (it treats the date as a number). Click on the exclamation mark and a menu appears suggesting that the date is included in the calculation. If you choose this option, the calculation will be wrong, of course. Excel will then display another error message, advising that the adjacent calculations should be similarly amended.

MODIFYING ERROR INDICATORS (EXCEL 2002-2016)

The way Excel displays Error Indicators can be modified, which is useful if you are preparing data for a presentation or report, or if you are importing data that contains several problems.

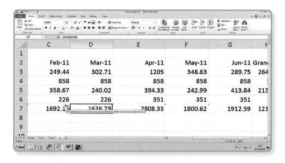

Above/right: The list of numbers shown here has a date at the top with a Sum total at the bottom; Excel sees the date as a number and suggests it should be included in the Sum total – if it is included, it then suggests that the adjacent calculations should be similarly amended.

Switch off the Error Indicator

The green Error Indicator triangle that appears in the top left corner of a cell when an error is identified can be switched off. In Excel 2002–2003:

→ **Click on the Tools menu**

→ **Choose Options**

→ **From the dialogue box that appears, select the Error Checking tab**

→ **Remove the tick mark against Enable background error checking**

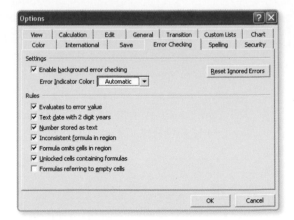

Above: Excel's Error Indicator and other error identification features can be modified in Excel 2002/2003 by clicking on the Tools menu, choosing Options and selecting the Error Checking tab from the dialogue box.

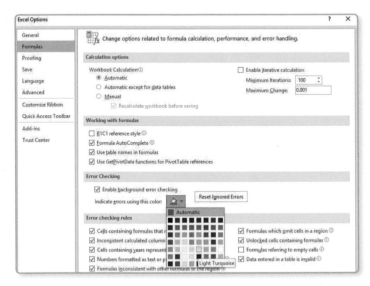

Above: The Error Indicator in Excel 2002–2016 can be switched on or off and its colour changed.

In Excel 2007–2016:

→ **Click on the Office button or File menu**

→ **Select Excel Options or Options**

→ **From the dialogue box that appears, select Formulas from the list on the left**

→ **Remove the tick mark against Enable background error checking**

Change the Error Indicator's Colour

The colour of the Error Indicator triangle can be changed. Open the Options dialogue box (see previous section for instructions) and return to where Error Checking can be switched on/off. The colour of the Error Indicator will be displayed next to this option. Click on the drop-down triangle to choose another colour (green is standard, but you may find red easier to see, for example).

CHANGING ERROR INDICATOR RULES

The part of the Options or Excel Options dialogue box where error checking can be modified includes a series of tick boxes under the Rules or Error Checking Rules, which can help to display or hide Error Indicators. Some of the useful options to switch on or off are:

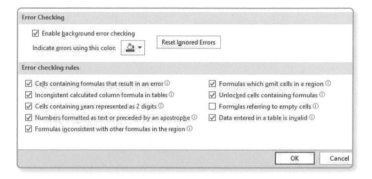

Above: Several options are available for changing Error Indicator rules; this feature was introduced in Excel 2002.

In Excel 2002–2003:

➔ **Number stored as text:** Imported data can sometimes be incorrectly opened in Excel, where numbers are formatted as text. Such a problem can lead to incorrect calculations, so an Error Indicator is useful here to highlight this.

➔ **Inconsistent formula in region:** If a table of data includes Sum totals along the bottom, for example, and one of these calculations is different from the rest, an error indicator will be displayed.

➔ **Formula omits cells in region:** A useful Error Indicator if a list of numbers is Sum totalled, but one or more cells have been accidentally omitted.

➔ **Unlocked cells containing formulas**: This Error Indicator may not be useful unless you plan to protect a worksheet. Instead, it can cause Error Indicators to appear in most calculations, warning that the cells are not locked and therefore not protected.

➔ **Formulas referring to empty cells**: This option is usually switched off, but it may be useful to activate when importing data with unwanted empty cells.

In Excel 2007–2016:

➔ **Number formatted as text or preceded by an apostrophe**: Imported data can sometimes be incorrectly opened in Excel, where numbers are formatted as text. Such a problem can lead to incorrect calculations, so an Error Indicator is useful to highlight this.

➔ **Formulas inconsistent with other formulas in the region**: If a table of data includes Sum totals along the bottom, for example, and one of these calculations is different from the rest, an Error Indicator will be displayed.

➔ **Formula which omits cells in a region**: A useful Error Indicator if a list of numbers is Sum totalled, but one or more cells have been accidentally omitted.

➔ **Unlocked cells containing formulas**: This Error Indicator may not be useful unless you plan to protect a worksheet. Instead, it can cause Error Indicators to appear in most calculations, warning that the cells are not locked and therefore not protected.

➔ **Formulas referring to empty cells**: This option is usually switched off, but it may be useful to activate when importing data with unwanted empty cells.

Hot Tip

Error Indicators can often be difficult to understand until you see them on screen.

DATA INPUT CHECKS

The contents of cells can be checked when the data is being typed, after it has been imported or at a later date. It is essential to check your data to reduce the chance of errors creeping in and ensure the accuracy of results given in the spreadsheet.

DATA VALIDATION

You can check data as you are typing it into a cell using the Data Validation feature, which enables error messages to be displayed instantly and rules set to ensure the correct type of data is entered.

Setting up Data Validation

Choose the cell or range of cells where data will be input and where rules restricting what type of data can be entered will prove helpful. In Excel 2003 and earlier versions, click on the Data menu and choose Validation. In Excel 2007–2016, click on the Data ribbon tab and select the Data Validation ribbon button. In all cases, a Data Validation dialogue box will appear on screen.

Above: Data Validation can be set to ensure only dates are entered in a cell; the dates can also be restricted to ensure they are not too old or too far in the future.

Setting the Data Validation Rule

Select the Settings tab in the Data Validation dialogue box, then click on the drop-down arrow next to the white box with the option Any value. A list of Data Validation rules will appear. Rules including Whole number, Decimal, Date, Time and Text length allow values greater than, less than, equal to or between ranges to be entered. Choose a type of value, then select a condition (greater than, less than) and specify a value or the values for the rule.

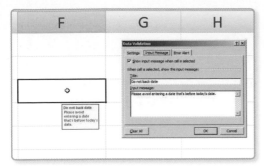

Above: A Data Validation message can be set to appear on screen so you know what type of information should be input in the cell you have selected.

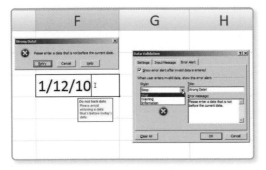

Above: An error message can be set to appear on screen whenever the wrong type of data is entered into a cell.

Hot Tip

Data Validation input messages can be removed from the screen by returning to the dialogue box and removing the tick mark against the option labelled 'Show input message when cell is selected'.

Hot Tip

If a date entered into a cell must not be backdated, create a Data Validation rule allowing a date with a condition of greater than or equal to. In the Start date box, enter the function =Today().

Displaying a Message on Screen

Click on the Input Message tab in the Data Validation dialogue box to set up an on-screen message alert when one of the cells containing the Data Validation rule is selected. Type a few words in the small white box underneath the label Title. This will appear at the top of the message box. In the larger white box underneath Input Message, type a longer and more informative explanation of what type of data should be entered.

Displaying an Error Message

Select the Error Alert tab in the Data Validation dialogue box. Choose a style of error alert by clicking on the drop-down triangle. The Stop style prevents the wrong type of data from being entered, whereas Warning and Information styles will display an error, but allow it to be overruled. Type a title for the error alert box and a message to be displayed. Click on OK to close the Data Validation dialogue box and test the rule.

STEP-BY-STEP: USING DATA VALIDATION TO CREATE A DROP-DOWN LIST

Creating a drop-down list was covered in Chapter 5, but instead of inputting data, a drop-down list can be used where only values or text on the list can be selected, thus avoiding data errors. The following step-by-step guide shows how to set up this Data Validation rule.

1   Create a list of the data you want to appear on the drop-down list. Display it away from the cells to be included in the drop-down list to ensure it won't be deleted by accident.

2   Select the cells that will use the drop-down list. In Excel 2007–2016, click on the Data ribbon tab and select the Data Validation button. In earlier versions of Excel, click on the Data menu and choose Validation. In the dialogue box, make sure the Settings tab is selected.

3   Choose List from the drop-down list beneath Allow. Click inside the Source box, then select the cells containing the list created in step 1. Click on the Input Message tab and the Error Alert tab to set up any messages, then click on OK to close the dialogue box.

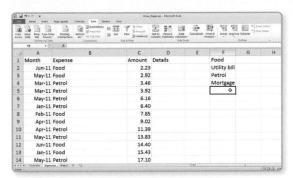

Above: Create a sample list of entries for the Data Validation drop-down list.

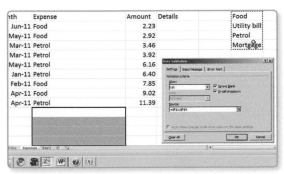

Above: Select the cells to which the drop-down list will apply, open the Data Validation dialogue box and set up the list.

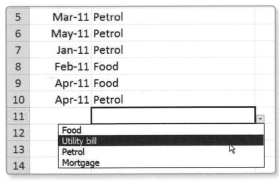

Above: After setting up the Data Validation for a list, click inside one of the cells and check whether a list appears.

4   Test the Data Validation rule works by selecting any of the cells from step 2. A drop-down list should appear (you may need to click on the drop-down triangle attached to the selected cell). Select an item from the list and it will be entered into the cell.

Hot Tip

Data Validation can be removed from a cell or range of cells by selecting them, returning to the Data Validation dialogue box and clicking on the Clear All button.

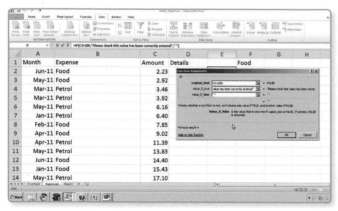

Above: An IF function can be used to check inputted values and display a message if any of them are greater than a specific amount.

Hot Tip

The IF function can be combined with other functions to help identify errors.

IF CHECKS

The IF function can be used to check the values or contents of cells to search for errors. This can be useful for checking inputted data while it is being entered or afterwards, or for checking through imported data.

Searching for Mistyped High Values

If a value is entered with too many digits, it can cause serious confusion and, of course, inaccurate results. An IF function can help reduce the risk of such an error occurring. For example, a list of household expenses could use an IF function to display an error if a petrol expense exceeds £100 or a food expense is greater than £200. The function would not amend the mistyped data, but would display a message on screen.

EXACT MATCHING

The Exact function checks two cells to see if they are similar and displays a TRUE or FALSE statement. This is useful for comparing sales results, for example, where weekly or monthly results are imported and compared in a table. The structure of the results is usually the same every month, with the same listing of product codes in the same order, so the data can be easily copied over and compared in a summary table. However, if the order of product codes is changed, then it is not always so easy to spot the changes. This is where the Exact function can help.

Creating an Exact Function

The illustration shows sales results for four product codes in January and February. This data has been copied into Excel and eventually the sales figures will be copied into a month-by-month table. On initial inspection, it looks like the product codes listed in

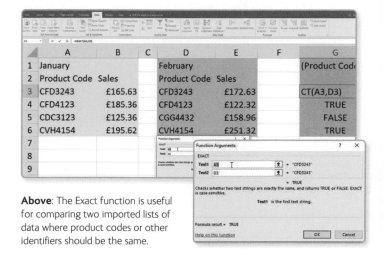

Above: The Exact function is useful for comparing two imported lists of data where product codes or other identifiers should be the same.

column A are the same as in column D. However, using the Exact function reveals that the product codes in row 5 are different. The Exact function is created by clicking on the fx toolbar or formula bar button. It is located in the Text category of functions and can be set up as shown in the illustration.

HIDING ERRORS

Errors, blank cells and zero values can be hidden to help tidy up a report or a presentation.

Hiding Errors in PivotTables

Right-click inside a PivotTable and choose PivotTable Options or Options from the menu. A PivotTable Options dialogue box will appear. In Excel 2007–2016, select the Layout & Format

Above: Errors and empty cells in PivotTables can be replaced with values or meaningful text to help tidy up the data.

tab. In all cases, there are two options here that allow values or text to be entered for errors or empty cells. Add a tick mark to an option to be able to enter a number or text in its corresponding box.

Hiding Errors with Conditional Formatting (2007–2016)

A function such as a Vlookup may display an error message if it cannot retrieve the data it is asked to look for. When this happens, Conditional Formatting can be used to hide the error by changing the colour of the text to match the cell's fill colour. The step-by-step guide below can use the Excel_Exercises.xls spreadsheet available on www.flametreepublishing.com/samples. Once opened, select the Vlookup worksheet.

STEP-BY-STEP: SETTING UP CONDITIONAL FORMATTING TO HIDE ERRORS (2007–2016)

1   Select the cell or cells containing functions that may display errors. Click on the Home ribbon tab and select the Conditional Formatting button. From the menu that drops down, select Manage Rules at the bottom of the list.

2   The Conditional Formatting Rules Manager dialogue box will appear on screen. Click on the option near the top left corner, labelled New Rule. A New Formatting Rule dialogue box will open.

3   From the list at the top of the New Formatting Rule dialogue box, select the second one down, labelled 'Format only cells that contain'. In the lower half of the dialogue box (under

the title 'Format only cells with:'), click on the drop-down triangle next to Cell Value, and choose Errors from the list.

4   A new Conditional Formatting rule has been established to format cells containing errors. All that's left to do is choose the formatting, so click on the Format button near the bottom of the dialogue box. A Format Cells dialogue box will appear. Choose a matching font and fill colour to ensure errors cannot be seen. Click on OK to return to the first dialogue box.

5   Click on OK to set up the Conditional Formatting rule and return to the first dialogue box, where this rule will now be listed. Click on OK to close this dialogue box and return to the spreadsheet. Test the Conditional Formatting rule by forcing an error to be displayed. The illustrations here show Conditional Formatting applied to a Vlookup, so if a town/city is entered in F1 that cannot be found, the Vlookup's error is hidden in cell F2.

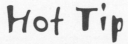

Hot Tip
Conditional Formatting can be used to hide any type of unwanted data by making the font and fill colour of a cell the same.

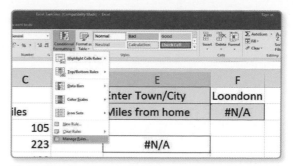

Above: Function errors can be hidden using Conditional Formatting.

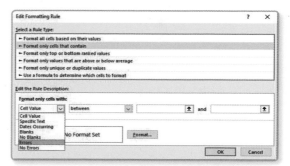

Above: Conditional Formatting in Excel 2007–2016 can be set up to format cells containing errors by creating a new rule.

Above: Conditional Formatting has been applied to the Vlookup in cell F2 to change the cell text to yellow if an error is displayed – the lookup value in cell F1 here has been misspelled.

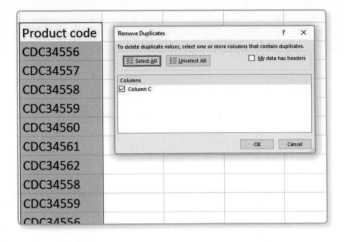

Left: Duplicate data can be deleted from lists in Excel 2007–2016 based on one or more columns.

DELETING DUPLICATES

Imported data can sometimes be repeated, resulting in duplicate entries. Excel 2007–2016 have a Remove Duplicates feature, which can help to delete the extra unwanted data.

Remove Duplicates (2007-2016)

Select the entire list containing duplicate entries. Click on the Data ribbon tab and select the Remove Duplicates button. A Remove Duplicates dialogue box will appear on screen. A tick box in the top right corner stipulates whether the list has headers at the top (headings). If the list has headings, they will be displayed with tick boxes against them. Add tick marks to the columns where duplicate entries should be deleted if found. Click on OK and a message box will appear telling you how many duplicate entries were deleted.

> ## Hot Tip
> Save a copy of your Excel file before removing duplicates, just in case you want to return to the original data.

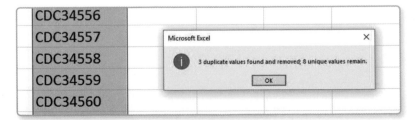

Left: After removing duplicates in Excel 2007–2016, a message box will appear showing how many duplicate values have been found and removed.

UNIQUE RECORDS

Listed data can be trimmed by filtering only unique records. This is useful for refining imported data where duplicates may exist, or locating data input errors where the same records have been accidentally entered twice. Unique Record filtering can be found in Advanced Filtering.

Hot Tip

After advanced filtering to show unique records only, all the data can be displayed by clicking on the Data menu, selecting Filter and choosing Show All. In Excel 2016, select Clear on the Sort & Filter section of the Data ribbon.

Filtering for Unique Records

This method requires data to be listed, ideally with headings across the top. Select all the data, including the headings. Click on the Data menu or ribbon tab and select Advanced, or Filter followed by Advanced Filter. Make sure the cell references for the List range are correct in the small dialogue box that appears. Add a tick mark to the option in the bottom left corner, labelled Unique records only. The list can be filtered in place without deleting any data, so keep this option selected and click on OK. The row numbers will be displayed in blue, indicating they have been filtered.

Above: Excel's Advanced Filter allows unique records to be filtered, which hides duplicated data.

ANALYSING ERRORS

Errors can be analysed and resolved in Excel with the use of several tools. The most useful and commonly used of these error-analysis tools is the Formula Auditing toolbar.

FORMULA AUDITING

Formula Auditing tools can help to trace the cells used in a calculation and evaluate a calculation containing an error. In Excel 2003 and earlier versions, there is a Formula Auditing toolbar, which is opened by clicking on the Tools menu, selecting Auditing or Formula Auditing and choosing Show Auditing Toolbar from the sub-menu. In Excel 2007–2016, click on the Formulas ribbon tab and the Formula Auditing buttons are displayed near the top right of the screen.

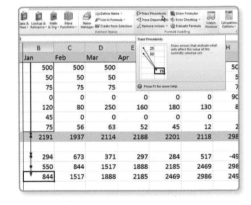

Above: Trace Precedents reveals which cells affect a calculation.

Trace Precedents

Trace Precedents is useful for seeing which cells have been used to create a calculation, and this feature works best if a cell containing a calculation is

Left: This cash-flow forecast shows that cell B23 (amount spent on clothes in January) affects several calculations throughout the spreadsheet and is also linked to another workbook.

Hot Tip

Click on Remove Arrows to remove any lines and arrows from the spreadsheet that were created by Trace Precedents and/or Dependents.

selected. Click on Trace Precedents to display lines and arrows from the cells that affect the selected cell. Continue clicking on Trace Precedents to trace further back.

Trace Dependents

A cell containing a value might be used in a calculation and this can be found by selecting it and clicking on Trace Dependents. Continue clicking here to see the knock-on effect from one calculation to another. This is especially useful in a cash-flow forecast.

Links to Other Worksheets or Workbooks

When tracing precedents or dependents, if a cell is connected to another cell contained in another workbook or worksheet, a black dotted line with an arrow will be displayed with a small box. Double click on the arrow's dotted line to open a Go To box and see which workbook or worksheet the cell is linked to. To open the worksheet or workbook, select it in the Go To box and click on OK.

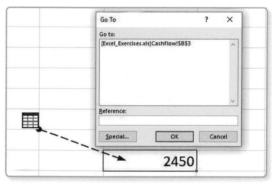

Above: When tracing precedents or dependents, a link to another worksheet or workbook is displayed with a dotted arrow – double-click on the line to open a Go To box and open the respective worksheet or workbook.

Trace an Error

A cell containing an error can sometimes be quickly fixed using Trace Error. This has the same effect as clicking on Trace Precedents, and will illustrate any cells that may be causing the error.

In Excel 2003 and earlier versions, Trace Error can be found on the Formula Auditing toolbar and looks like an exclamation mark inside a yellow diamond. In Excel 2007–2016, click on the Formulas ribbon tab, select the drop-down triangle next to the Error Checking button (within the Formula Auditing section of the ribbon) and choose Trace Error from the drop-down list.

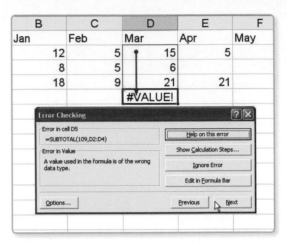

B	C	D	E	F
Jan	Feb	Mar	Apr	May
12	5	15	5	
8	5	6		
18	9	21	21	
		#VALUE!		

Error Checking

Errors in an entire worksheet can be found by clicking on the Error Checking toolbar button (a yellow diamond containing a tick mark) in Excel 2003 and earlier versions, or by clicking on Error Checking on the Formulas ribbon tab in Excel 2007–2016. A dialogue box will appear and if any errors are identified, they will be displayed in turn

Above: An entire worksheet can be checked for errors – any errors that are discovered are instantly analysed and solutions offered.

with an analysis of the problem and suggestions on how to resolve each one. Excel does not find cells containing error values such as #N/A or #NAME? but does try to resolve cells with #VALUE! errors.

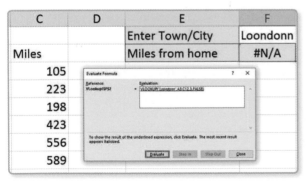

C	D	E	F
		Enter Town/City	Loondonn
Miles		Miles from home	#N/A
105			
223			
198			
423			
556			
589			

Above: An error in a calculation can be evaluated to help analyse every part of it and see where the problem lies.

Evaluate a Formula

Calculations (formulas) can be evaluated to help analyse the cell references used and locate the problem. Select the cell containing the error and, in Excel 2007–2016, select Evaluate Formula from the Formulas data ribbon. In earlier versions of Excel, click on the Evaluate Formula button on the Formula Auditing toolbar (looks like a large magnifying glass with the letters fx inside). An Evaluate Formula dialogue box will appear. Click on the Evaluate and Step In buttons to analyse the calculation and find the problem.

EXCEL TROUBLESHOOTER

Like any computer program, Excel is not perfect. It can generate several problems that are simply traits of the software. Other problems are usually down to user error. The following pages cover some of the typical troubles people experience when using Excel.

CELL, COLUMN AND ROW ERRORS

When a cell's content is not displayed as it should be, there is usually a good reason and a fairly simple solution.

Date Turns into a Number

Excel stores dates as sequential serial numbers – so they can be used in calculations to work out differences between dates, for example. 1 January 1900, for instance, is serial number 1. 1 January 2008 is serial number 39,448 because it is 39,448 days after 1 January 1900. Sometimes a cell will have been formatted as a number, so when a date is entered into it, that date is converted to its serial number equivalent. This problem can be fixed by right clicking inside the cell and choosing Format Cells. From the dialogue box that appears, select the Number tab, the Date option on the left and choose a date format.

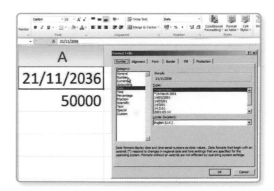

Above: Cells containing date formatting will convert a number into a date: here, cell A1 has been formatted as a date, so when the number 50,000 is input, the number is converted to a date.

Number Turns into a Date

In this case, a cell has been formatted as a date, so when a number is entered into it, that number is converted into a date. For example, 50,000 will become 21 November 2036. This can be fixed by right-clicking inside the cell and choosing Format Cells. From the dialogue box that appears, select the Number tab, choose the Number option from the left and click on a format on the right.

Copied Calculations Don't Work

If a copied calculation refers to the same cell in each calculation, the reference to

Hot Tip

In Excel 2007–2016, a cell can be quickly formatted to a date, number or other type by clicking on the Home ribbon tab and selecting from the drop-down list of formats at the top of the screen.

that cell must be fixed with dollar signs (e.g. B8). The illustration shows a calculation for cost of work in column E, based on a fixed daily rate of £100 (in B8), and a list of days worked in column D. The first calculation in E2 reads =D2*B8, but when copied down, the next calculation reads =E3*B9, which is wrong (there's nothing in B9). Writing the first calculation as =E2*B8 will fix this problem. Copy the calculation down and the reference to B8 will not change.

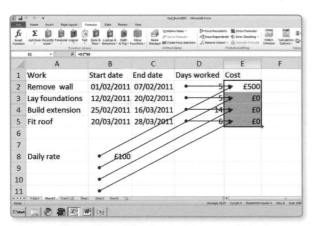

Above: The calculation copied down in cell E2 will not work unless the reference to B8 is fixed with $ signs.

Copied Data is Incorrectly Formatted

This problem often occurs when copying data from another program or from a website into Excel. The pasted data may be too narrow for the columns, or it may be in the wrong font and size. In Excel 2002 and later versions, click on the Smart Tag at the bottom right corner of the pasted cells. A menu will appear offering options for changing the format of the cells. In earlier versions of Excel, undo the pasting (Ctrl+Z on the keyboard), click on the Edit menu and choose Paste Special. Try one of the options in this dialogue box and click on OK. It may require several attempts to find the best format.

Moving Dotted Lines around a Cell or Group of Cells

Moving dotted lines around a cell or range of cells signifies that they have either been copied or copied using Format Painter. If you don't intend to make use of this copying, press Escape on the keyboard to switch it off.

Blue Row Numbers with Missing Rows

If one or several row numbers are blue and some of them are missing, they have been filtered using

AutoFilter, Filter or Advanced Filtering. In Excel 2007–2016, click on the Data ribbon tab and click on the Clear button on the Sort & Filter section (top middle of the screen). In earlier versions of Excel, click on the Data menu, choose Filter and select Show All from the sub-menu.

Missing Rows or Columns (pre-2007)

If some rows and/or columns are missing and there are + and – buttons at the side or across the top of the worksheet, along with numbered buttons in the top left corner of the worksheet, the active spreadsheet has either been Grouped (Outlined) or Subtotalled. First, click on the Data menu, select Group and Outline and from the sub-menu, choose Clear Outline (if available). Otherwise, click on the Data menu, choose Subtotals and then select Remove All from the dialogue box that appears.

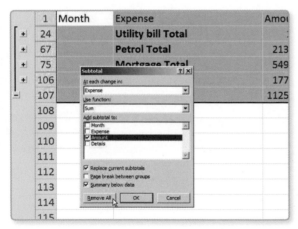

Above: If Subtotals have been applied to a worksheet a number of rows may be missing, but these can be retrieved by opening the Subtotals dialogue box and selecting the Remove All button.

Missing Rows or Columns (2007-2016)

If some rows and/or columns are missing and there are + and – buttons at the side or across the top of the worksheet, along with numbered buttons in the top left corner of the worksheet, the active spreadsheet has either been Grouped (Outlined) or Subtotalled. In Excel 2007–2016, click on the Data ribbon tab and select the drop-down triangle under the Ungroup button (top right corner of the screen). If Clear Outline is available from the drop-down menu, choose it. Otherwise, click on the Subtotal button and select the Remove All button from the dialogue box that appears.

Hidden Rows or Columns

If some rows or columns are missing and there are no + and – boxes down the side or along the top, or any blue row numbers, then the missing rows or columns are probably hidden.

Hot Tip

Missing rows or columns can also be revealed by selecting the rows/columns on either side of the missing ones, right-clicking and choosing Column Width or Row Height. In the box that appears enter number 15 and click on OK.

4	Mar-11	Utility bill
5	Apr-11	Utility bill
14	Jan-11	Utility bill
15	✂ Cut	Utility bill
16	📋 Copy	Utility bill
17	📋 Paste Options:	Utility bill
18	Paste Special...	Utility bill
19	Insert	Utility bill
20	Delete	Utility bill
21	Clear Contents	Utility bill
22	Format Cells...	Utility bill
	Row Height...	Utility bill
	Hide	Utility bill
	Unhide	Utility bill

|◄ ◄ ► ►| PivotTable   **Expenses**   Sheet2   IF

Right: Hidden rows or columns can be unhidden by selecting the rows or columns on either side, right-clicking and choosing Unhide.

These can be unhidden by selecting the rows or columns on either side of those that are hidden (hold the left button down on the mouse and swipe over the column letters or row numbers). Right-click inside the selected rows or columns and choose Unhide from the shortcut menu that appears.

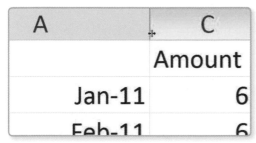

Above: Sometimes the width of a column or height of a row has been reduced so much that it disappears from the screen.

Compressed Rows or Columns

Sometimes the height of a row or width of a column is accidentally reduced to the point that it cannot be seen. If you have tried all the solutions above for retrieving missing rows and columns, then hover the mouse pointer over the row numbers or column letters where the row or column is missing. The mouse pointer will be a cross with two arrows, but if the line of its cross changes to two lines, the missing row or column has been found. When this happens, hold the left button down on the mouse and move down the screen to increase the missing row's height or to the right to widen the missing column.

SCREEN LAYOUT PROBLEMS

The Excel screen can become very frustrating if toolbars and menus disappear, or other features cannot be found. Here are a few of the most common problems and their solutions.

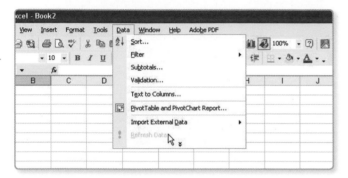

Above: The menus in Excel 2000–2003 only list the recently used options, but you can expand the menu by positioning the mouse pointer over the double arrows at the bottom.

Short Menus (2000–2003)

In Excel 2000, 2002 and 2003, the menus (File, Edit, View, etc.) are often shorter than they should be because they only list the recently used options. If a particular option is missing, move the mouse pointer down to the bottom of the menu and hover it over the downward-pointing double arrows. The menu will be extended to reveal all its options.

Missing Ribbon (2007–2016)

Excel 2007–2016 use ribbons with sets of buttons based on each ribbon tab (File, Home, Formulas, etc.). If the ribbon buttons are missing but the ribbon tabs can be seen, the ribbon has been minimized or collapsed. Right-click on any of the ribbon tabs and a shortcut menu will appear with a tick mark against Minimize the Ribbon or Collapse the Ribbon. Select this option to remove the tick mark and reveal the ribbon and its buttons.

Hot Tip

Excel 2010 displays a small arrow in the top right corner of the screen, which can be used to minimize and maximize the ribbon.

Lost Toolbars (pre-2007)

Right-click on any toolbar button or menu option and a checklist of toolbars will appear. If the toolbar required does not have a tick mark against it, select it and it will appear on screen.

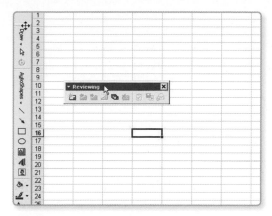

Above: Toolbars in Excel 2003 and earlier versions can be moved around the screen and displayed around the edges or floated on top of the cells.

Toolbars in the Wrong Place (pre-2007)

If a toolbar is in the middle of the screen, hover the tip of the mouse pointer over its title bar (along the top), hold the left button down and move the toolbar to the correct location. If a toolbar is incorrectly positioned around an edge of the screen, look for an embossed line or two lines on the side of the toolbar. Position the tip of the mouse pointer over this line or lines, hold the left button down and move the mouse to move the toolbar.

Toolbars Side by Side (pre-2007)

Sometimes two toolbars can be displayed on the same row, which means that several buttons may be missing. However, the toolbars can be separated. In Excel 2002 and 2003, click on the small button between the two toolbars, which looks like two arrows and a drop-down triangle. From the menu that appears, select Show Buttons on Two Rows. In earlier versions of Excel, find the point at which the two toolbars are divided and look for an embossed line or two lines to drag and drop one of the toolbars below the other one.

Hot Tip

Toolbars in Excel 2003 and earlier versions can be moved and positioned around the screen. They will snap into the edges of the screen or can float on top of the cells.

Excel Upgrades

Excel 2007–2016 can seem confusing when used for the first time, especially if you've upgraded from Excel 2003 or an earlier version. The menus have been replaced with ribbon

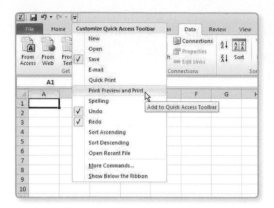

Above: Upgrading to Excel 2007–2016 from an earlier version can be frustrating at first, but most of the old features are still easy to find.

tabs along the top of the screen, displaying different sets of buttons. Most of the familiar Excel features can be found via these ribbon tabs and buttons, however. There is also a Quick Access Toolbar in the top left corner of the screen, which can be customized to add or remove buttons.

Task Pane Trouble (2002–2003)

Excel 2002 and 2003 have a Task Pane, displayed on the right side of the screen, which includes various options for opening files, copying data and inserting ClipArt (Excel 2003 has more options than 2002). This Task Pane can be displayed or hidden by clicking on the View menu and selecting Task Pane.

Missing Cells and Page 1 Displayed across the Worksheet

This suggests that Page Break Preview has been selected in error. Page Break Preview shows the number of pages that will be printed and which cells will be included on each page. It also hides rows and columns that will not be printed. To

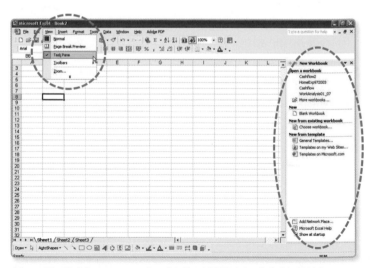

Above: The Task Pane was introduced in Excel 2002 and included in 2003, but phased out in 2007; it can be displayed and removed by clicking on the View menu.

return to the standard view of the spreadsheet, click on the View ribbon tab in Excel 2007–2016 and select the Normal button near the top left of the screen. In earlier versions of Excel, click on the View menu and choose Normal.

FILE TROUBLE

Excel files can disappear from the screen, refuse to open in later versions of the program or display worrying warnings about compatibility. Below are some of the most common file problems – and how to solve them.

Above: In Page Break Preview the spreadsheet can look confusing and unfamiliar, so select Normal to fix the view.

Where Are Recently Opened Files?

When two or more Excel files are opened, some of them will not be visible on the screen, but they are still open. Click on the View ribbon tab in Excel 2007–2016 and select the Switch Windows ribbon button near the top right of the screen. A list of open Excel files will be displayed. Simply select one to view it. In Excel 2003 and earlier versions, click on the Window menu and a list of open Excel files will be displayed at the bottom of the menu. Select one to view it.

Hot Tip

Hold down the Alt key on the keyboard and press the Tab key to switch between programs and files.

Saving Down

An Excel file can be 'saved down' as an earlier file type, so that it can be opened in previous versions of Excel. In Excel 2007–2016, for example, a file can be saved as an Excel 97–2003 type. However, when the file is resaved (Ctrl+S on the keyboard), a warning box may appear on screen if Excel identifies some features that may not work in an older version of the program. Click on Copy to New Sheet to save this information, or click on Continue to ignore the warning.

Above: Saving an Excel file for use with an earlier version of the program can cause a warning message to appear; the file can still be opened in an older version of Excel, but some features may not be available.

Wrong File Format

Files created in Excel 2007–2016 have a .xlsx extension, whereas files created in older versions have a .xls extension. These newer .xlsx files can be opened in older versions of Excel (2000, 2002 and 2003) by downloading a compatibility pack available at http://support.microsoft.com/kb/924074. Alternatively, ask the person who created the .xlxs file to save it as an Excel 97–2003 or earlier version.

Cells Cannot Be Changed

This usually means that the worksheet has been 'protected' to prevent the data from being amended or deleted (although it may still be possible to edit some of the cells). To remove the protection feature in Excel 2007–2016, right-click on the open sheet tab at the bottom left corner of the screen and see if the words Unprotect Sheet are displayed on the shortcut menu. If they are, select this option and if a box does not appear requesting a password, the sheet has been unprotected and all the cells can be edited. In Excel pre-2007, click on the Tools menu, choose Protection and select Unprotect Sheet.

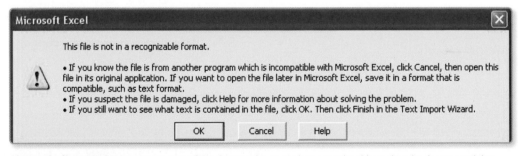

Above: If a file created in a newer version of Excel cannot be opened, you may be able to download a compatibility pack (for Excel 2000, 2002 and 2003).

AFRAID TO ASK

Many questions about Excel might seem too simple to ask, but the truth is that sometimes the simple things are overlooked and are never fully explained. Below are some of the most common 'afraid-to-ask' questions raised during Excel training courses.

WORKSHEETS, ROWS AND COLUMNS

The terminology of workbooks, worksheets, rows and columns quickly becomes assumed knowledge among groups of people using Excel, but there are many simple questions that you may not know the answers to.

How Do I Name a Sheet Tab?

Right-click on the sheet tab in the bottom left corner of the screen and choose Rename. Type a name for it and press Enter/Return on the keyboard. Alternatively, double-click on the sheet tab and you will be able to rename it.

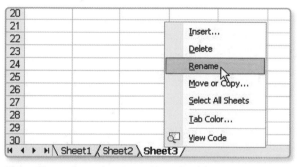

Above: Sheet tabs can be renamed by right clicking on each one and selecting Rename from the shortcut menu that appears.

Hot Tip

Insert an extra worksheet by holding down the Shift key on the keyboard and pressing F11.

Can I Add More Sheets to a Workbook?

Yes. In Excel 2003 and earlier versions, click on the Insert menu and choose Worksheet. In Excel 2007–2016, click on the small Insert Worksheet button to the right of the sheet tabs.

Why Are There So Many Rows and Columns?

It's hard to think why anyone would need more than one million rows in a worksheet in Excel 2010–2016, but long lists of data can sometimes use all this space. When these rows and columns are empty, they don't take up much space on the computer, so the size of the file isn't a problem.

Can I Reduce or Increase the Number of Rows and Columns?

The number of rows and columns cannot be changed. The amount available is fixed according to the version of Excel in use. For example, Excel 97 has 65,536 rows, whereas Excel 2010–2016 has 1,048,576 rows.

CELLS AND CALCULATIONS

It is easy to pick up bad habits when selecting cells, copying data and making calculations. Here are some ways to help you establish best-practice methods.

Above: Check the shape of the mouse pointer before selecting cells with the mouse – it must be a white cross; if it's a small black cross, the selected cells will be copied.

Why Do Cells Sometimes Move and Sometimes Copy When Selected?

Pay attention to the mouse pointer. If it's a white cross, this can be used for selecting cells. If it's a white arrow, it will move a cell or group of cells. If it's a small black cross, it will copy or Autofill the contents of a cell.

Can a Calculation Start with a + Symbol?

Some of the early spreadsheet programs (such as Quattro Pro) created calculations by starting with a + symbol, and this is also possible in Excel, but it is best practice to start with an = symbol. In most versions of Excel, an = symbol will be automatically inserted at the beginning of the calculation. So if you create the calculation +A1+A2, Excel will convert this to read =+A1+A2.

Can I Type Calculation Values from the Cells Rather Than Cell References?

Typing the cell values won't give you an incorrect calculation, but if those cell values change, the calculation won't change. Including cell references in a calculation (e.g. =A4-F4) allows the calculation to be automatically updated if the values in cells A4 and F4 change.

	A	B	C
1		Jan	Feb
28	Misc	75	
29	Total Expenses	2191	1!
30			
31	Surplus/Deficit	294	
32	Opening Balance	◊ 550	
33	Closing Balance	+B31+B32	1!
34			

Above: A calculation can start with a + symbol, but Excel will add an = symbol to the beginning of it, so it's best practice simply to start with this.

Should All Calculations Start with =Sum?

It is possible to write a calculation where cells are multiplied, divided, subtracted and added using =Sum, but this is the wrong use of the function and is not necessary. The calculation =Sum(A1*A2), for example, can be written more efficiently as =A1*A2.

Above: A calculation can go wrong if you don't press Enter/Return on the keyboard to finish, but instead click elsewhere in another cell.

Can I just Click in Another Cell When I've Finished in the First?

In most cases it will be fine, but if a calculation is being written, upon clicking in another cell, that cell reference will be included in the calculation. It is always better to press Enter/Return on the keyboard.

EXTRA PRACTICE

EXCEL EXERCISES

Once you've got to grips with Excel it's best to get in some practice on all the different features and functions it offers. The following pages cover a variety of task-based, step-by-step guides on creating spreadsheets for specific purposes. For sample worksheets, visit www.flametreepublishing. com/samples and download the Excel_Exercises.xls workbook.

STEP-BY-STEP: MONTHLY EXPENSES LIST

A monthly expenses list can be useful for keeping a record of household, work or business expenditure. The following guide explains how to create a simple list and includes details of additional features covered in earlier chapters that can be applied to it. If you want to save time typing, select the Expenses worksheet on the Excel_Exercises.xls workbook mentioned above.

1   Using a new workbook and worksheet, enter the heading 'Month' in cell A1, 'Expense' in cell B1, 'Amount' in cell C1 and 'Details' in cell D1. In cell A2, enter a month and year, such as Jan 11, or Aug 12. Maintain this format for all dates to ensure continuity.

2   Enter several months and years in column A. In column B, enter an expense type such as petrol, supermarket, clothes, utility bill, insurance or mortgage. Remain consistent with the types of expenses.

3   Enter some amounts in column C to correspond with the expenses listed in columns A and B. If necessary, enter some further details in column D. For example, a utility bill could include details such as 'water rates' or 'gas' in column D.

4   Save the Excel file with a meaningful name, such as 'Expenses'. Select one cell inside the list, click on the Data menu or ribbon and choose the Sort menu option or button (Excel

2007–2016). The Sort dialogue box will appear. Choose to sort on Month or Expense, then click on OK to see the data sorted.

5   More expenses can be added to the list and Excel's AutoComplete saves time on typing expense entries. For example, type the letter U at the bottom of the list in column B and utility bill will appear (if it has already been entered above). Press Enter to confirm the AutoComplete suggestion.

	A	B	C	D
1	Month	Expense	Amount	Details
2	Feb-11	Mortgage	858	
3	Feb-11	Utility bill	65	Water rates
4	Mar-11	Petrol	20.78	
5	Apr-11	Utility bill	65	Water rates
6	May-11	Utility bill	65	Gas

Above: Enter a series of headings across the top of the worksheet and several sample expenses down the columns.

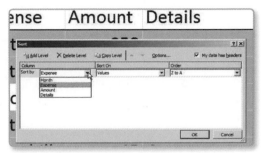

Above: The expenses list can be sorted on month, expense type and amount.

	A	B	C
98	Mar-11	Food	97.72
99	Jun-11	Food	98.34
100	Apr-11	Food	98.97
101	May-11	Food	123.30
102	Jun-11	Food	
103			

Above: Excel AutoCompletes the expense entries in column B, which saves time on repeatedly typing them.

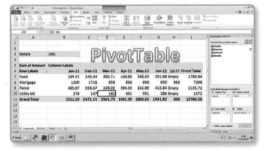

Above: An expenses list can be further analysed, converting it into a PivotTable with summarized data and totals.

Extra Excel Features

→ **Subtotals**: Sort and group the data to see subtotals per month and by expense type. See page 119 (Chapter 3) for further details and more exercises.

→ **PivotTable:** Group and tally the expenses data into a simple-to-read table with totals. See page 122 (Chapter 3) for more information and another step-by-step guide.

→ **Drop-down list:** Expenses can be entered into this spreadsheet using a drop-down list (Data Validation). See Adding Drop Down Variables on page 182 (Chapter 5).

→ **Highlight high-value expenses:** Use Conditional Formatting to change the colour of high-value expenses. See page 90 in Chapter 2 for more information.

→ **AutoFilter or Filter:** Filter the list so that only specific types of expenses are displayed, expenses for particular months, or values under or over a certain amount. For further details on AutoFilter, see Manipulating Long Lists on page 109 (Chapter 3).

STEP-BY-STEP: DOWNLOADING A BANK STATEMENT

Most financial institutions provide online banking with the facility to download account statements. The following guide provides an outline of what's typically involved in downloading and opening a statement in Excel.

1   When viewing an account online with a financial institution (e.g. a bank or building society), look for an option to download a bank statement. You may be able to stipulate a start and end date for the statement, or just a particular month.

2   When choosing to download a statement, there may be several choices of file types to download. If Excel isn't available, look for comma separated values (CSV) or Text (TXT) instead.

3   If it's not possible to download a bank statement, try selecting the transactions online, right-clicking and choosing Copy. Open Excel, right-click in an empty cell and choose Paste to transfer the copied data.

Above: Most online accounts have a facility to download statements.

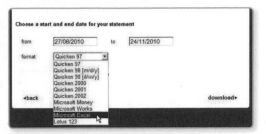

Above: Online accounts statements can usually be downloaded in a variety of formats.

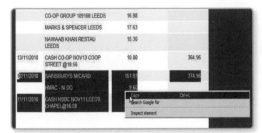

Above: If a statement cannot be downloaded, try selecting the transactions, right-clicking and choosing Copy.

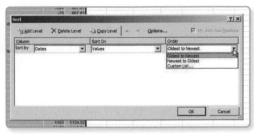

Above: Downloaded statement transactions may need to be sorted.

4 If a statement has been saved as an Excel or compatible file, open Excel and press Ctrl and the letter O on the keyboard to open a file. Change the file type (near the bottom of the dialogue box) to All Files. Locate the downloaded statement and click on Open.

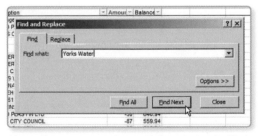

Above: Transactions can be quickly found using the Find box – press Ctrl and F to open this search box.

5 If Excel can understand the structure of the statement it will open it; if not, a Text Import Wizard will appear (see Chapter 3 for more details on this feature). Widen any columns that are too narrow.

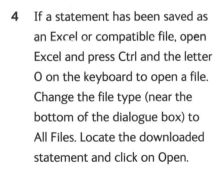

6   Check the date order of the transactions is correct (e.g. oldest transactions at the top). If it isn't, select all of the data, then click on the Data menu or ribbon and choose Sort. From the dialogue box that appears, select the Date column and choose to sort ascending or oldest to newest, for example. Click on OK to return to the spreadsheet and sort the data.

7   Transactions can be quickly found, which helps with checking receipts. Hold down the Ctrl key on the keyboard and press the letter F. A Find box will appear. Enter a word or amount to search for, then click on Find Next.

8   Further data can be added to this bank statement. A separate statement will need to be downloaded, but the data can be selected and copied from it, then pasted into the older statement.

Extra Excel Features

➔   **Highlight overdrawn balances**: Use Conditional Formatting to change the colour of overdrawn balances. See page 90 (Chapter 2) for more information.

➔   **Downloading text files**: Excel can open statements that are saved as text or CSV files. See the section on Long Lists on page 105 (Chapter 3) to find out about importing text files.

STEP-BY-STEP: CALCULATING A LOAN

Excel can be used to speculate loans and investments with varying amounts, interest rates and years. The following guide shows how to create a loan calculation using a PMT function. The completed worksheet can be found in the Excel file (Excel_Exercises.xls) that is used with this book, in the PMT_Loan worksheet. For more details see page 152.

1   Using a blank worksheet, enter the title 'Amount to borrow' in cell A1, 'Number of repayments' in cell A2, 'Interest rate' in cell A3, 'Amount of repayment' in cell A4 and ' Total repaid' in cell A5.

2 Select cell B1 and enter the negative value -10000. In cell B2, enter the number 48 and in cell B3, enter 5.6%.

	A	B
1	Amount to borrow	-10000
2	Number of repayments	48
3	Interest rate	5.60%
4	Amount of repayment	
5	Total repaid	
6		

Above: Enter the details as shown to be able to use the PMT function and calculate the amount of each repayment.

3 Select cell B4 and click on the fx button on the toolbar or formula bar (depending on the version of Excel being used). From the function dialogue box that appears, select or change the category to Financial and choose PMT from the list of functions. Click on OK.

	B	C	D	E
	-10000			
	48			
	5.60%			
	12,B2,B1)			

Above: Complete the criteria for the PMT function to allow Excel to calculate the value of each repayment based on the values displayed in cells B1, B2 and B3.

4 In the PMT Function Arguments dialogue box, select the first white box (Rate) and enter B3/12. In the second white box (Nper), enter B2 and in the third white box (Pv), enter B1. Click on OK to return to the spreadsheet.

5 Select cell B5 and enter the calculation =B4*B2. This will calculate the total amount repaid. Test the PMT function by changing the values in cells B1, B2 and B3.

	A	B
1	Amount to borrow	-15000
2	Number of repayments	60
3	Interest rate	7.50%
4	Amount of repayment	£300.57
5	Total repaid	£18,034.15

Above: Change the values in cells B1, B2 and B3, and the PMT function will automatically calculate a new repayment amount.

FURTHER READING

Albright, S.C., Winston, W. & Zappe, C., Data Analysis and Decision Making with Microsoft Excel, South-Western College Publishing, 2008.

Alexander, M. & Walkenbach, J., Excel Dashboards and Reports, John Wiley & Sons, 2010.

Arthur, E., Excel Made Easy, Arcturus Publishing Ltd, 2009.

Crews, T. & Murphy, C., CaseGrader: Microsoft Office Excel 2007 Casebook with Autograding Technology, Course Technology, 2007.

Day, Alastair, Mastering Financial Modelling in Microsoft Excel: A Practicioner's Guide to Applied Corporate Finance, Financial Times/ Prentice Hall, 2007.

Few, S., Show Me the Numbers: Designing Tables and Graphs to Enlighten, Analytics Press, 2004.

Frye, C., Excel 2007 Step by Step, Microsoft Press, 2007.

Gottfried, B.S., Spreadsheet Tools for Engineers: Excel, McGraw-Hill Higher Education, 2002.

Hart-Davis, G., How to Do Everything with Microsoft Office Excel 2003, McGraw-Hill Osborne, 2003.

Jelen, B., Microsoft Excel 2010 in Depth, QUE, 2010.

Koneman, P.A., Advanced Projects for Microsoft Excel 2000, Prentice Hall, 2000.

MacDonald, M., Excel 2010: The Missing Manual, O'Reilly Media, 2010.

Murray, K., Microsoft Office 2010 Plain and Simple, Microsoft Press, 2010.

Person, R., Balanced Scorecards and Operational Dashboards with Microsoft Excel, John Wiley & Sons,

Rendell, I. & Mott, J., Advanced Spreadsheet Projects in Excel, Hodder Education, 2008, 2008.

Russ, M. & Ferrari, A., Microsoft PowerPivot for Excel 2010: Give Your Data Meaning, Microsoft Press, 2010.

Salkind, N.J., Statistics for People Who (Think They) Hate Statistics: Excel 2007 Edition, Sage Publications, Inc, 2009.

Schmuller, J., Statistical Analysis with Excel For Dummies, For Dummies, 2009.

Smith, K.T., Smith, L.T. & and Smith, L.C., Microsoft Excel for Accounting: Auditing and Accounting Information Systems, Prentice Hall, 2002.

Walkenback, J., Excel VBA Programming for Dummies, John Wiley & Sons, 2010.

WEBSITES

www.excelbanter.com
A forum that focuses only on Excel and Excel-related topics.

www.excel-easy.com
A clearly broken down tutorial on Excel with lots of examples and links to further information in each chapter.

www.excelforum.com
A discussions forum where you can share advice and get help from other members of the community, as well as support from Excel experts. Includes What's New in Excel and Excel Tips and Tutorials.

www.excelfunctions.net
This site provides information and help on, and examples of each of, Excel's built-in functions, along with how to perform popular tasks using a combinations of these functions and/or the mathematical operators to create formulas.

www.exceltip.com
Tips on how to use Excel for data management, calculations and other business-related tasks. Also has Excel consultants and experts available to answer questions.

www.functionx.com/excel
Lessons on how to use the 2007 version of Excel to create spreadsheets, perform calculation and carry out data analysis.

www.microsoft.com/learning
Microsoft-certified online courses to learn valuable skills on various Microsoft products.

www.mrexcel.com
Support and wide range of services for Excel.

https://support.office.com/en-us/excel
Microsoft's official website for help and troubleshooting covering past and current versions of Excel.

www.ozgrid.com/Excel
A list of Excel formulas, plus tips and tricks on how to use them.

www.spreadsheetpage.com
Sells Excel-related programs as well as having free tips and downloads on Excel.

INDEX